EVERYDAY *Mexican* INSTANT POT® COOKBOOK

REGIONAL
CLASSICS
MADE
Fast & Simple

EVERYDAY
Mexican
INSTANT POT®
COOKBOOK

Leslie Limón

PHOTOGRAPHY BY NADINE GREEFF

ROCKRIDGE
PRESS

Designer: Merideth Harte
Editor: Kim Suarez
Production Editor: Andrew Yackira
Photography © Nadine Greeff, p. 25 © Hélène Dujardin; food styling by Tami Hardeman
Map illustration by Merideth Harte

ISBN: Print 978-1-64152-219-9 | eBook 978-1-64152-220-5

Dedication

To Hope, Nick, Ashley, and Jack for always believing in their mom and adding flavor to my life. I love you forever and always.

CONTENTS

INTRODUCTION

It's no secret that I love Mexican food. It's the food I grew up eating, having been raised by my Mexican grandparents. It's the food I continue to enjoy and make for my family, and it's the new-to-me foods that I discovered during the 18 years I lived in Mexico. And really, what's not to love? Mexican food has become one of the most popular cuisines in America, and with very good reason: It's absolutely delicious and so easy to make.

Mexican food is more than just tacos though. It's hearty soups and stews like menudo and pozole. It's roasted meats like Cochinita Pibil (page 114) and *barbacoa*. It's rich one-pot meals—also known as *guisados*—like *bistec ranchero*. It's traditional staples like *frijoles charros* and Mexican rice. It's sweet, comforting desserts like *arroz con leche*. But it's also modern Tex-Mex and Cal-Mex twists to the classics like Mole Pulled Pork Sliders (page 119) and Chile Relleno Chowder (page 61). These are just a few of the dishes you'll learn to make from this book.

While more and more people are choosing to make Mexican cuisine at home, the majority of Americans get their Mexican food fix from dining out at taquerias, fast-food chains, and restaurants. Albeit tasty and satisfying on the spot, most of the food in chains and restaurants is either fried, greasy, covered in cheese, or full of unnecessary fat and sodium.

But that doesn't have to be the case. You can make delicious Mexican food at home that is not only healthy and full of flavor, but also quick and easy. The Instant Pot® lets you do just that because it locks in the flavor and the nutrients of whatever you're cooking.

The Instant Pot® is not your *abuelita's* (grandma's) pressure cooker! I used to be so afraid of my grandmother's pressure cooker—which she often used to cook beans or shredded beef for her famous tamales—because of the constant hissing and wobbling of that little knob that seemed to get louder and louder as it boiled away on the stove. Because I've tested and retested every recipe in this book to bring you authentic Mexican flavor and incorporate real-user best practices specifically for the appliance, I now know that there is nothing to fear when using an electric pressure cooker.

If you already own an Instant Pot® and are looking for new foods to prepare, or if you just want to re-create the dishes that you always order from your favorite Mexican restaurant but are feeling intimidated by certain ingredients, this is the cookbook for you. The *Everyday Mexican Instant Pot® Cookbook* teaches you how to make everything from salsas to rice and beans to desserts, and everything in between. And if you have some extra time, the last recipe chapter features simple, essential staples like homemade Corn Tortillas (page 132), refreshing Pico de Gallo Verde (page 135), and Fruity Agua Fresca (page 140) that don't require an Instant Pot® to help you prepare a proper Mexican feast your *abuelita* would approve.

ARROZ CON POLLO, PAGE 78

CHAPTER 1

Mexican Food Fast & Easy

"The Instant Pot® works magic on ingredients
that are common to the Mexican table—be it
fresh or dried chiles, garlic, meats, or beans.
It makes humble ingredients downright special.
It frankly makes them sing."

I learned about the finer points of Mexican food firsthand when I moved from Southern California to a town two hours north of Guadalajara. There, in the heart of Mexico, my *suegra* (mother-in-law) taught me to cook traditional Mexican dishes. Even beforehand, though, some of my earliest childhood memories are of watching my grandmother make homemade flour tortillas and her storied shredded pork tamales, and my *abuelito* (grandpa)—the family baker—drying *orejones de manzana* (apple slices) to make empanadas and *capirotada* (bread pudding). Collectively, it all left its mark.

Fast-forward to the present day. With three hungry teens and a college student, time is of the essence. Just as important is the need to put healthy, hearty food on the table. Enter my electric pressure cooker (a.k.a. the Instant Pot®). This indispensable kitchen tool lets me coax out layers of flavor in no time flat, and it ensures that I get homemade meals on the table while supporting my passion for authentic Mexican fare.

Whether you are new to the electric pressure cooker, don't own one yet, or consider yourself an Instant Pot® whiz, these recipes are for you. The scent of rich, slow-cooked Mexican classics—and interpretations of my own—will waft through your home while you make the most of your time and energy.

The Traditions of Mexican Cooking & Pressure Cooking

Pressure cooking is nothing new in Mexican kitchens. In fact, home cooks have relied on the power of pressure cooking for generations for comforting and hearty dishes, such as soul-stirring soups and stews, pots of toothsome ranchero beans, and—everyone's favorite—carnitas.

From rural kitchens, where much cooking occurs over an open flame, to urban homes countrywide, I've learned this: The more things change, the more they stay the same. Thousands of years after chiles, maize, and squash were domesticated, many of the same ancient cooking tools—like the *cazuela*, metate, *molcajete*, and comal—are employed to this day.

Admittedly, everyone is abuzz about electric pressure cookers these days—and with good reason. For starters, they've come a long way, offering a bevy of self-regulating safety features, including sensors to monitor temperature and amount of pressure. However, they're nothing new in the Mexican kitchen, really, where pressure cookers have remained in regular rotation.

Yes, the electric pressure cooker is a more modern addition to Mexican kitchens, but by no means is pressure cooking new. That said, the benefit is clear: You simply plug it in, tap a button, and it goes to work. Just as user-friendly as a slow cooker, this time-saving appliance has an added benefit: It effectively gets dinner on the table a full day sooner, supporting modern cooks' need for time management and convenience.

Add to that the fact that it works magic on ingredients that are common to the Mexican table, be it fresh or dried chiles, garlic, meats, or beans. It makes humble ingredients downright special. It frankly makes them *sing*.

Moreover, an electric pressure cooker combines flavors effectively. Whereas complex Mexican stews once required a clay *cazuela* for simmering the sauce and a pressure cooker for tenderizing meat before they were combined to meld flavors, an electric pressure cooker effectively does both, all at once! The results are rich, layered, and commingled dishes. Really, they speak for themselves.

An electric pressure cooker even works wonders on cooked salsas, ones that can be spooned over eggs, scooped up with chips, or used to blanket enchiladas. Need to

MEXICAN FOOD IS HEALTHY FOOD

Mexican food sometimes gets a bad rap from those who consider it to be greasy fast food. I'm here to say that's a misnomer. Authentic Mexican food is more than just tacos and quesadillas—much, much more. The cuisine reflects both the vast diversity of the people who created it and the land that's teeming with natural resources. In reality, true Mexican cuisine capitalizes on the country's abundance of fresh produce, and it's time that those not in the know take stock. Fortunately, an electric pressure cooker has the power to help cooks break out of the standard Mexican repertoire served in Americanized Mexican restaurants. Before you know it, you'll be making Tacos de Rajas con Crema (page 64) with the best of them!

I'd also suggest thinking about ways you can turn healthy ingredients, like lentils, into a Mexican-inspired feast, just like I have with Lentil Picadillo (page 66). Or substituting vegetables for fattier proteins, as I do with Cauliflower Tinga (page 65). At the end of the day, the sky is the limit. You just need to master the pressure cooker and a handful of Mexican pantry essentials.

make rice and beans in a flash? How about rice pudding? Good news: The Instant Pot®
has your back.

Further, given Mexican cuisine's penchant for using tougher cuts of meat, the
electric pressure cooker is a godsend. When such a cut of meat is cooked in an ample
amount of sauce, the pressure cooker breaks down the protein's chewy fibers, yielding
fork-tender, melt-in-your-mouth results.

That's true whether you're tackling *birria* (shredded meat that has been slow
roasted in an underground pit and is served in a flavorful chile-infused sauce) or
beef tongue tacos.

The Mexican Pantry

To make things easy on yourself, stock your pantry with basic ingredients and tools.
That way, cooking Mexican food can become an effortless part of your routine.

HERBS AND SPICES

Allspice: These peppercorn-like berries are commonly toasted and ground to add
warmth to salsas, moles, and stews. Save time by buying them already ground.

Bay leaves: Mexican bay laurel is used to infuse marinades, soups, and stews
with flavor.

Cilantro: Used generously in Mexican cuisine, this annual appears in everything
from salsa to rice dishes, soups, and moles. Even though fresh is best, do keep dried
cilantro in your pantry to use in a pinch. Note: Many of the recipes in this book
call for cilantro sprigs. These are edible, but some people prefer to remove them
before serving.

Cinnamon: Mexican cinnamon, also called Ceylon cinnamon, is warm and fragrant.
It's sold both as sticks and ground.

Cumin: Strong and toasty cumin seeds are sold both ground and whole. In the case
of the latter, they should be toasted.

Oregano: The Mexican variety of this herb is frequently used dried in dishes like
pozole and tomato-based soups.

Sesame seeds: An essential ingredient in moles, these nutty seeds also show up in baked goods, such as bread.

Thyme: This aromatic herb is often used to pickle vegetables, as well as to flavor slow-simmered dishes, like stew.

BEANS

Black beans: Also called black turtle beans, this small, shiny, dark purple–to-black variety is rich and meaty tasting, making it a popular choice to use in vegetarian chili and as *frijoles refritos* (refried beans) in burritos.

Flor de Mayo beans: Native to Mexico and known for their outstanding flavor, these small bush beans range in color from lilac to purplish to tan.

Mayocoba beans: Originally from Peru, these mild, buttery beans are medium in size and pale yellow in color. They're often used in soups, as well as to make refried beans.

Peruano beans: Light cream, buff, or yellow in color, these mild-tasting, creamy beans originated in the Peruvian Andes and can be used in dishes calling for navy, cannellini, or pinto beans.

Pinto beans: Eaten whole, in burritos, in broth, and mashed and refried, pinto beans are the most common bean variety used in Mexican cuisine.

See page 144–145 for a cooking chart for beans and grains.

GRAINS

Corn: Used to make tortillas, tostadas, tamales, *tlacoyos*, crunchy tortilla chips, and iconic *elotes*, this staple ingredient is integral to Mexican cooking.

Flour: The basis for flour tortillas—and crowd-pleasers like quesadillas—flour is also essential to many Mexican baked goods, including sandwich rolls and cookies.

White rice: Whether you crave *horchata*, *arroz* (rice), or *arroz rojo* (red rice), this pantry staple is prevalent in Mexican cuisine.

PACKAGED, BOTTLED, CANNED

Achiote: Orange-red seeds from this tropical shrub or small tree are commonly used in Yucatan cuisine, particularly pork and chicken dishes.

Canned beans: High in fiber and extra quick when you're in a time crunch, canned beans come in lots of varieties. Use ones that are low in sodium so you can salt dishes your way.

Canned tomatoes: Keep these on hand to make quick salsas, sauces, soups, and stews. Fire-roasted tomatoes add another excellent layer of flavor.

Chipotles en adobo: These smoked and dried jalapeños are reconstituted and canned in a tangy, spiced tomato, vinegar and garlic purée.

Chocolate: Sold in round bricks, Mexican chocolate is sweetened with extra sugar and spiced with cinnamon, and it's used to flavor drinks—such as *chocolate de agua* and *champurrado* (both types of Mexican hot chocolate)—as well as some moles.

Dried chiles: A variety of dried chiles—such as ancho, guajillo, and chiles de árbol—are imperative to have in your culinary toolbox. Use them for everything from enchilada sauce to salsas.

Hot sauce: Add heat to your dishes with some of the many Mexican hot sauces, such as Tapatío, Valentino, Cholula, and El Yucateco's Salsa Picante de Chile Habanero, of which there are several kinds.

Lard: This fat of choice in Mexican kitchens was first introduced by the Spanish. It's used for making flour tortillas and tamales and frying masa-based snacks, and is essential to the preparation of carnitas and *chicharrón*.

Pepitas: These pumpkin seeds can be ground and used as a thickener for moles and other sauces, and are a common ingredient in Mexican candies. They're also eaten as a snack while still in their hulls. Meanwhile, in central Mexico, they're peeled and used to make sweet, puffed amaranth bars called *alegrías*.

Tortillas: Keep packaged flour and corn tortillas on hand. When you have time, make your own, using the recipe Tortillas de Maís (page 132)

Vinegar: White and apple cider vinegars are used to pickle vegetables, make vinaigrettes, and add nuance to one-pot meals.

Essential Equipment

A well-stocked Mexican kitchen needs a few basic tools. Here's what I suggest.

A kitchen thermometer is important to have on hand for checking the internal temperature of meat. A probe with a remote display makes things easier still.

Kitchen tongs come in handy when cooking in a deep electric pressure cooker, enabling you to turn and toss ingredients effortlessly.

A ladle is essential for serving chili, soups, and stews directly from your Instant Pot®. Look for one with a wide, shallow bowl.

Silicone oven mitts help when it comes time to lift the inner pot in and out of your electric pressure cooker. They also protect your fingers from hot steam burns during the pressure release phase.

A flexible spatula lets you turn and flip ingredients in the event they get stuck. Look for one that's made of silicone for the best results.

NICE TO HAVE

Having an extra inner pot is helpful when you don't want to do dishes in between, but are looking to cook more than one Instant Pot® dish for a meal.

A fat separator—while not required—is helpful when it comes time to strain sauces and cooking liquids. Simply pour liquid into the vessel, watch the fat rise to the top, and pour the defatted liquid back into your electric pressure cooker to thicken, reduce, or blend into a sauce.

A tempered glass lid is beneficial when you're sautéing or slow cooking items in an electric pressure cooker.

FAQs

Whether or not you've used an electric pressure cooker before, I know you might have questions. It's fair. I want it to be easy for you to make as many recipes as possible, so I've included some common questions and offered answers and solutions based on my experience.

1. Periodically, my electric pressure cooker makes a ticking or popping sound. Why?
   Unless the bottom of the inner pot was wet when you began cooking (it should be dry), this is normal! You'll hear a tick or light cracking sound when the power switches or when pressure expands when it's changing temperature.

2. My Instant Pot® is hissing and spitting out steam while coming to pressure. Is this normal?
   As long as the pressure release handle is in the "sealing" position and you have enough liquid in your pot, this is normal. You can expect to see steam coming out of the pressure release (a.k.a. steam release) handle or float valve. Give it some time and your Instant Pot® float valve will rise up and the pot will be pressurized.

3. I just can't get my rice to have the right consistency. What's happening?
   If your rice is too hard either you need more water or the rice didn't cook long enough. In the case of the former, adjust the water ratio according to the recipe. If you open the lid too early, put it back on and let the rice sit for 5 minutes or so after the cooking cycle completes.

4. If I double a recipe, do I double the cook time?
   No, the actual cook time is the same. Just be aware it could take a little longer for the appliance to come to pressure.

5. Are there foods that don't work well in an electric pressure cooker?
   Foods like noodles can foam, froth, and sputter, ultimately clogging the appliance. Other foods that can cause excess pressure include applesauce, rhubarb, cranberries, split peas, oatmeal, and other cereals. Remember, too, that pressure cookers add moisture, so don't expect crispy foods—as well as baked goods made with dough like phyllo—to turn out right. Finally, delicate foods, like certain types of fish, may not yield the results you're looking for.

6. What are the best foods to cook in an Instant Pot®?
   Nothing beats beans, soups, stews, and meats that require slow cooking, since the appliance significantly reduces cooking time.

7. Can I use my electric pressure cooker for canning?

It can be used for boiled-water canning, though altitude may affect the cooking temperature. However, do not use your pressure cooker for pressure canning. Refer to the USDA Complete Guide to Pressure Canning for complete canning guidelines.

8. Why is it taking my pressure cooker so long to come to pressure?

This is impacted by a variety of factors, including how much you have in the pot. A fuller pot takes longer to come to pressure. Also, the type of food that's in the pot can affect timing (liquid foods take longer to come to pressure than dense ones).

9. Is an electric pressure cooker actually capable of baking?

It's not an oven, so it's technically not baking anything. But you can cook baked goods, such as cakes or quick breads, this way. Just be aware that they're getting steamed, not baked. They will, however, cook up light and fluffy.

10. Can I cook foods from frozen?

You can, though I don't recommend it. If you opt to cook them, be aware that it'll take longer for the pot to come to pressure. Plus, it works better to cook items that have been frozen in a flat layer rather than big chunks (or roasts). When the pot does come to temperature, the cooking time is the same.

11. What's the difference between natural pressure release and quick pressure release?

When your pot finishes its cooking cycle, it beeps to let you know. At this point, most recipes tell you to release pressure naturally (which occurs gradually), release pressure quickly, or do a combination of both.

12. How do I clean my electric pressure cooker?

The cooker base houses the heating element, so you need to avoid getting it wet. Never place your Instant Pot® in the dishwasher. Instead, clean the exterior of the cooking base with a damp cloth, and use a slightly damp cloth to clean the interior of the cooker. That said, the inner pot of the cooker (the stainless steel cooking pot), the lid, the sealing ring, and the steam rack can be washed by hand and generally also can be washed in the dishwasher.

13. Should I be worried about safety?

This generation of electric pressure cookers has many built-in safety mechanisms. Even if you forget to add liquid, it'll shut off and display an error code.

14. How should I store my Instant Pot®?

Unplug it after each use. Store it on the counter, in the cabinet, or wherever you have space. Just be sure to store the inner lid upside down on the inner pot. This way, it'll be able to air out.

The Recipes

In this cookbook, you'll find a solid, quality collection of Mexican electric pressure cooker recipes, ones brimming with authentic flavors. All the while, they're recipes that fully utilize the multifunctional features of the appliance.

REGIONAL CUISINES

Mexican cuisine is hyper-regional and beloved not only in Mexico, but also in many parts of the United States, where Mexican cuisine spreads from border states like Texas to other southwestern states—and well beyond.

MEXICO

In northern and northeastern Mexico ("El Norte")—an area that includes Baja, Sonora, Chihuahua, and Durango—the cuisine features a bevy of grilled beef dishes mixed with green chile, and quince, which makes its way into desserts. This region is also Mexico's major cheese producer, turning out queso fresco; Monterey Jack–like ranchero; mild, creamy *cuajada*; ricotta-esque *requesón*; semisoft queso *menonita* (also called Chihuahua cheese); and several varieties of smoky *asadero*.

Not surprisingly, the Gulf Shore sees its share of fresh seafood, with iconic dishes like lime-laced ceviche and dishes made from red snapper, like *huachinango a la veracruzana*. Here, Afro-Cuban, Spanish, and Creole influences shine.

Likewise, the seafood game is strong along the Yucatán Peninsula, where storied, achiote-laced *cochinita pibil* also reigns. This area is also marked by the use of habaneros and tropical fruits, among them tamarind, mamey, avocados, bitter oranges, and plums. Often, food is wrapped in banana leaves and cooked in a pit oven. This region's Mayan food is inflected with influences from Cuba and other Caribbean islands, as well as Middle Eastern, Asian, and European cultures.

On the Pacific shore, Manzanillo fishermen are known for their seafood chowders brimming with squid, oysters, shrimp, clams, and octopus. The Pacific north—Sinaloa, Jalisco, Nayarit, and Colima—are credited with birria (particularly in Guadalajara), as well as menudo and a range of pork dishes.

Meanwhile, moles hail from the Isthmus states, as they rely on the region's chocolate supply. Oaxacan cuisine is based on staples like corn, chiles, and beans, though it's fabled for its seven mole varieties: *coloradito* (little red), *negro* (black), *amarillo* (yellow), *chichilo* (smoky stew), *rojo* (red), *manchamanteles* (tablecloth stainer), and *verde* (green).

Because Puebla's population is varied, its dishes are distinct from the rest of Mexico. As a result, you'll encounter roasted peppers stuffed with a mix of nuts, fruits, and ground meat. Central Mexico—and Mexico City, in particular—favors street foods, such as carnitas, tortas, and tacos. Needless to say, the city is known for haute Mexican fare, while at the same time embracing regional dishes from across the country. Beyond that, you'll also find spots specializing in pre-Hispanic food, including insect-based dishes.

If you particularly love Mexican snacks (*antojos*), you have Mexico's central plains to thank, since tacos, tostadas, and quesadillas with salsa and guacamole are particularly beloved in this region.

I welcome you to travel around Mexico and the United States within the pages of this cookbook—no plane ticket required.

UNITED STATES

Southwestern and Tex-Mex cuisine—a fusion of Mexican and American fare—comes from creations of Tejanos and is found most readily (and authentically) throughout Texas and states such as Arizona, New Mexico, Colorado, Utah, and Nevada. Expect dishes like chili con carne, hard-shell tacos, and fajitas, as well as ingredients like shredded cheese and flour tortillas.

Cali-Mex: Thank the Mexican state of Baja California in northern Mexico, as well as its large Chinese population, for this distinct regional cuisine. There are dishes from this area you won't find elsewhere, the sometimes surprising, Baja-style dishes nonetheless loaded with peppers, onions, and chiles.

FEATURES

The recipes in this book were developed to be practical and easy to follow, with clear, concise steps that help you prepare flavorful, healthy favorites in your electric pressure cooker, fuss-free.

TIME

You'll find useful instructional labels that help you make the most of your pressure cooker's multifunctional settings and capabilities with ease. This includes prep time, time under pressure, pressure release method, and total time for every pressure cooker recipe.

Regional Map of Mexican Cuisine

Mexican cuisine is highly regional, with some areas focusing on distinct dishes, such as rich moles, fresh-plucked seafood and antojos (snacks).

NEVADA

UTAH

COLORADO

TEX-MEX

CALIFORNIA

MEXI-CALI

ARIZONA

NEW MEXICO

BAJA CALIFORNIA

SONORA

TEXAS

THE GULF SHORE

THE NORTH

CHIHUAHUA

COAHUILA

SINALOA

DURANGO

NUEVO LEÓN

ZACATECAS

TAMAULIPAS

SANTIAGO DE QUERÉTARO

THE YUCATÁN PENINSULA

HIDALGO

SAN LUIS POTOSÍ

TLAXCALA

THE PACIFIC SHORE

NAYARIT

MEXICO CITY

YUCATÁN

QUINTANA ROO

AGUASCALIENTES

JALISCO

THE ISTHMUS STATES

GUANAJUATO

COLIMA

MICHOACÁN

VERACRUZ

PUEBLA

CAMPECHE

CENTRAL PLAINS

GUERRERO

OAXACA

TABASCO

CHIAPAS

INGREDIENTS

Ingredients lists reflect the everyday items in a Mexican pantry, all of which are relatively easy to find or obtain. Some of the dried-good items, like beans, might already be in your pantry.

INSTRUCTIONS

Step-by-step instructions are easy to follow and clearly indicate cooking settings—just the thing for those who are new to the appliance.

LABELS

I've included different labels for different lifestyles and diets, and schedules, too.

30 Minutes or Less: These dishes can be prepared from start to finish within 30 minutes, making them ideal for weeknight dinners.

Kid-Friendly: When you're looking to feed the whole family—kids included—turn to these all-ages-approved preparations.

Dairy-Free: Whether you're lactose-intolerant or opt to eat dairy-free, look to this label for pitch-perfect preps throughout the book.

Gluten-Free: Those who are sensitive or allergic to gluten will find plenty of dishes to satisfy their cravings. (Always check ingredient packaging for gluten-free labeling.)

Vegan: This designation refers to satisfying plant-based dishes that are free of meat and animal by-products.

Vegetarian: Want to skip the meat? Many Mexican dishes are vegetable-based. Look for this label to find them in a flash.

TIPS

Look for recipe-specific tips for every recipe. These include what to do with leftovers, ways to repurpose ingredients, ingredient tips, Instant Pot® tidbits, substitution recommendations, and advice on what you can make ahead.

CLASSIC TOMATILLO AND ÁRBOL CHILE SALSA, PAGE 18

CHAPTER 2

Salsas & Sauces

Caldillo de Jitomate

MEXICAN TOMATO SALSA

PREP TIME: 5 minutes ✳ SAUTÉ: 8 minutes ✳ MANUAL: 30 minutes on high pressure
RELEASE: Quick ✳ TOTAL TIME: 45 minutes ✳ MAKES: about 8 cups

A common misconception about Mexican food is that all Mexican salsas have to be super spicy. This is not the case at all. For example, this Caldillo de Jitomate is a mild tomato salsa that can be spooned over everything from tamales and scrambled eggs to *entomatadas* (tomato enchiladas) and burritos. Or you can stir this into your favorite soups like *albóndigas*. This recipe yields a large batch of salsa, which you can store for up to a week in the refrigerator or up to 3 months in the freezer.

2 tablespoons vegetable oil
1 medium white onion, diced
3 garlic cloves, minced
3 pounds Roma tomatoes, quartered
1 teaspoon coarse salt, plus more for seasoning (optional)
2 bay leaves
1 teaspoon dried Mexican oregano, crushed

1. Set the Instant Pot® to Sauté and adjust to More for high. Heat the vegetable oil in the pot, then add the onion and sauté for 3 to 5 minutes, or until translucent. Add the garlic and sauté for an additional 30 to 60 seconds. Add the tomatoes, season with the salt, and sauté for about 2 minutes. Add ½ cup water, the bay leaves, and oregano.

2. Lock the lid into place and set the steam release valve to sealed. Select Manual and set the timer for 30 minutes on high.

3. When cooking is complete, quick release the pressure. Unlock and remove the lid.

4. Remove the bay leaves. Using an immersion blender, purée the salsa. Season with more salt, if necessary.

Freezer tip: Too much salsa? Allow it to cool completely, then divide into 1-cup portions and freeze in airtight containers. You can add the frozen salsa to soups or allow it to defrost overnight in refrigerator.

Queso Blanco Dip

PREP TIME: 5 minutes ✳ SAUTÉ: 3 minutes ✳ MANUAL: 10 minutes on high pressure

RELEASE: Quick ✳ TOTAL TIME: 20 minutes ✳ MAKES: 4 cups

Ever wish you could learn to make that creamy, delicious Queso Blanco Dip from your favorite Tex-Mex restaurant? This delectable appetizer is made with just a handful of ingredients: butter, fresh green chiles, Mexican crema, and an assortment of cheeses. You're going to love this homemade version so much that you'll no longer be impressed by the restaurant stuff. Just be sure to have a never-ending pile of tortilla chips on hand.

2 tablespoons butter

2 Anaheim chiles, seeded and finely chopped

2 fresh serrano chiles, finely chopped

1 garlic clove, minced

¾ cup Mexican crema or sour cream

½ cup whole milk

16 ounces Monterey Jack cheese, cut into bite-size cubes

10 ounces queso fresco, cut into bite-size cubes

½ teaspoon coarse salt, plus more for seasoning (optional)

½ teaspoon ground cumin

Tortilla chips, for serving

1. Set the Instant Pot® to Sauté and adjust to More for high. Heat the butter in the pot until completely melted. Add the chiles and garlic and sauté for 2 to 3 minutes. Stir in the Mexican crema and milk until well combined. Add the cheeses, salt, and cumin.

2. Lock the lid into place and set the steam release valve to sealed. Select Manual and set the timer for 10 minutes on high.

3. When cooking is complete, quick release the pressure. Unlock and remove the lid.

4. Gently stir the *dip* to combine. Season with more salt, if necessary. Ladle into a heat-proof bowl. Serve with tortilla chips.

Option tip: Stir leftover dip into cooked pasta for a Tex-Mex twist on macaroni and cheese!

Classic Tomatillo and Árbol Chile Salsa

PREP TIME: 5 minutes ✳ SAUTÉ: 3 minutes ✳ MANUAL: 12 minutes on high pressure
RELEASE: Quick ✳ TOTAL TIME: 20 minutes ✳ MAKES: 2½ to 3 cups

If I had to choose one salsa to eat for the rest of my life, it would be this one! Made with just tomatillos, garlic, and dried árbol chiles, this sauce can be served as a spicy appetizer with chips or pork rinds for dipping, atop your favorite tacos, or stirred into your favorite soups. Árbol chiles are my all-time favorite of all the dried chiles, because Yahualica—the small town in Mexico that I called home for 18 years—is famous for producing the best in the world.

1 tablespoon vegetable oil
40 dried árbol chiles, stems
    removed
3 garlic cloves, peeled
2¼ pounds tomatillos,
    husks removed
Coarse salt

1. Set the Instant Pot® to Sauté and adjust to More for high. Heat the vegetable oil in the pot, add the chiles and garlic, and sauté for 2 to 3 minutes, or until lightly toasted. Add the tomatillos and 2 cups water.

2. Lock the lid into place and set the steam release valve to sealed. Select Manual and set the timer for 12 minutes on high.

3. When cooking is complete, quick release the pressure. Unlock and remove the lid.

4. Using a slotted spoon, transfer the tomatillos, chiles, and garlic to a blender. Add 1 cup of the cooking liquid and process until smooth. Pour into a heat-proof bowl; season with coarse salt to taste.

Ingredient tip: For enhanced flavor, look for tomatillos *milperos*, a smaller, more flavorful variety, in the produce section of Hispanic grocery stores.

Nacho Cheese Sauce

PREP TIME: 5 minutes ✳ SAUTÉ: 1 minute ✳ MANUAL: 8 minutes on high pressure
RELEASE: Quick ✳ TOTAL TIME: 15 minutes ✳ MAKES: 5 cups

Host a nacho bar at your next get-together and wow your guests with this easy homemade nacho cheese sauce. The secret to this sauce is the tangy vinegar from the pickled jalapeños, which adds flavor and a little heat. Ladle this scrumptious sauce over tortilla chips or French fries, or serve it fondue-style with cubes of toasted bolillo rolls and fresh veggies for dipping.

1 tablespoon butter

¾ cup Mexican crema or sour cream

1 (12-ounce) can pickled jalapeño pepper slices, with their juices, plus more for garnish

2 pounds Cheddar cheese, cut into bite-size cubes

1. Set the Instant Pot® to Sauté and adjust to More for high. Heat the butter in the pot until completely melted. Stir in the Mexican crema and the jalapeño peppers and their juices. Add the cheese.

2. Lock the lid into place and set the steam release valve to sealed. Select Manual and set the timer for 8 minutes on high.

3. When cooking is complete, quick release the pressure. Unlock and remove the lid.

4. Stir the sauce gently to combine. Ladle over tortilla chips or French fries. Garnish with the pickled jalapeño slices.

Option tip: Crank the heat way up by stirring in ½ to ¾ cup of your favorite bottled hot sauce, such as Tapatío, Valentina, or Cholula.

Queso Fundido a la Cerveza

BOOZY QUESO FUNDIDO

PREP TIME: 5 minutes ✳ SAUTÉ: 10 minutes ✳ MANUAL: 10 minutes on high pressure
RELEASE: Natural ✳ TOTAL TIME: 25 minutes ✳ SERVES: 8

Need a fun appetizer to feed a crowd? Say *queso!* Queso Fundido to be exact. Often referred to as Mexican fondue, Queso Fundido is a tantalizing treat made with melted cheese. Traditionally it's made with just cheese and chorizo, but I like to add a little more flavor and depth to this dish with onion, garlic, chiles, mushrooms, and Mexican beer. Once the cheese has melted, serve Queso Fundido with tortilla chips for dipping or spoon onto warm tortillas.

1 tablespoon vegetable oil

8 ounces Mexican pork chorizo, casings removed

¼ medium white onion, thinly sliced

6 ounces sliced mushrooms

2 garlic cloves, minced

2 serrano chiles, finely chopped

2 Anaheim chiles, thinly sliced

⅓ cup Mexican crema or sour cream

1 (12-ounce) bottle Mexican beer, light or dark

2 cups shredded Colby Jack cheese

2 cups shredded white Cheddar cheese

1 cup shredded Oaxaca or mozzarella cheese

Coarse salt

Freshly ground black pepper

Tortilla chips or warm corn or flour tortillas, for serving (optional)

1. Set the Instant Pot® to Sauté and adjust to More for high. Heat the vegetable oil in the pot, add the chorizo, and fry for 5 to 7 minutes, or until cooked through.

2. Add the onion, mushrooms, garlic, and chiles. Sauté for about 3 minutes, or until the onion is translucent.

3. Stir in the Mexican crema, beer, and cheeses. Season lightly with coarse salt and pepper.

4. Lock the lid into place and set the steam release valve to sealed. Select Manual and set the timer for 10 minutes on high.

5. When cooking is complete, allow the pressure to release naturally. Unlock and remove the lid.

6. Stir gently to combine. Pour into a heat-proof bowl. Serve with tortilla chips or warm corn or flour tortillas.

Ingredient tip: Using a light-colored Mexican beer will add a soft, subtle flavor to the Queso Fundido, while a dark beer will add a bolder flavor.

Salsa de Chile Colorado

RED CHILE SALSA

PREP TIME: 10 minutes ✳ SAUTÉ: 3 minutes ✳ MANUAL: 10 minutes on high pressure
RELEASE: Quick ✳ TOTAL TIME: 25 minutes ✳ MAKES: 5 to 6 cups

This red chile sauce was a staple throughout my childhood. My *abuelito*, who was raised in the state of Chihuahua, always had cans of *chile colorado* in the pantry. Of course, this was back when dried chiles weren't as readily available as they are today. Making this sauce from scratch using dried chiles adds an earthy depth that you just can't get from a can.

2 tablespoons vegetable oil

8 ounces dried ancho chiles, stemmed and seeded

1 large white onion, coarsely chopped

8 garlic cloves, peeled

2 teaspoons coarse salt

1 teaspoon ground cumin

1 teaspoon dried Mexican oregano, crushed

1. Set the Instant Pot® to Sauté and adjust to More for high. Heat the vegetable oil in the pot, add the chiles, and sauté for 2 to 3 minutes, or until lightly toasted. Add the onion, garlic, and 4 cups of water.

2. Lock the lid into place and set the steam release valve to sealed. Select Manual and set the timer for 10 minutes on high.

3. When cooking is complete, quick release the pressure. Unlock and remove the lid.

4. Using an immersion blender, purée the chiles, onion, garlic, and cooking liquid until smooth. Season with the salt, cumin, and oregano.

Option tip: Transform this Salsa de Chile Colorado into *salsa de chile negro* by substituting 8 ounces of dried pasilla chiles for the anchos.

Salsa Gemma

GEMMA-STYLE SALSA

PREP TIME: 5 minutes ✳ SAUTÉ: 2 minute ✳ MANUAL: 12 minutes on high pressure
RELEASE: Quick ✳ TOTAL TIME: 20 minutes ✳ MAKES: 4 cups

Every once in a while you come across a sauce so rich and velvety, you wish you could just swim in it for hours or drink it like water. Salsa Gemma is that sauce for me. It's that good! Made with tomatoes, canned chipotle chiles, and an assortment of dried chiles, this sauce is traditionally served over a *torta gemma*—a type of torta *ahogada* (drowned sandwich) filled with pork carnitas that is popular in the state of Jalisco—but this sauce can be served over just about anything or stirred into your favorite soups.

1 tablespoon vegetable oil

4 dried ancho chiles, stemmed and seeded

2 dried guajillo chiles, stemmed and seeded

12 Roma tomatoes, quartered

4 to 6 canned chipotle chiles in adobo sauce

1 teaspoon coarse salt, plus more for seasoning (optional)

½ teaspoon freshly ground black pepper

1. Set the Instant Pot® to Sauté and adjust to More for high. Heat the vegetable oil in the pot, add the ancho and guajillo chiles, and sauté for 30 to 45 seconds per side.

2. Add the tomatoes, chipotle chiles, and 1½ cups water. Season with the salt and pepper.

3. Lock the lid into place and set the steam release valve to sealed. Select Manual and set the timer for 12 minutes on high.

4. When cooking is complete, quick release the pressure. Unlock and remove the lid.

5. Using an immersion blender, blender, or food processor, process all the ingredients together until smooth. Season with additional salt, if necessary.

Option tip: To make tortas *gemma*, fill lightly toasted bolillo rolls with Mexican crema, shredded pork carnitas, shredded lettuce, sliced tomato, and red onion. Slowly ladle about 1 cup of the warm Salsa Gemma over the tortas until completely drenched. Garnish with Mexican crema.

30 MINS OR LESS

DAIRY-FREE

GLUTEN-FREE

VEGAN

Salsa Ranchera

RANCH-STYLE SALSA

PREP TIME: 5 minutes ✳ MANUAL: 12 minutes on high pressure ✳ RELEASE: Quick

TOTAL TIME: 20 minutes ✳ MAKES: 3½ to 4 cups

If you've never made Mexican salsa at home before, this is the recipe to try. Salsa Ranchera is one of those salsas you always want to have in your refrigerator because you can serve it with tortilla chips or pork rinds for a quick appetizer, stir it into soups or *guisados* (one-pot dishes), drizzle it over tacos, or even spoon it over eggs for *huevos rancheros*. This ranch-style salsa—made with ripe Roma tomatoes, onion, garlic, and either fresh serrano chiles or jalapeño peppers—is sure to become an instant family favorite.

12 Roma tomatoes, cut in quarters

6 serrano chiles or jalapeño peppers, stemmed

4 garlic cloves, peeled

1 medium white onion, cut into large chunks

1½ teaspoons coarse salt, plus more for seasoning (optional)

⅓ cup fresh cilantro leaves

1. In the Instant Pot®, combine the tomatoes, chiles, garlic, and onion. Pour in 1 cup water and season with the salt.

2. Lock the lid into place and set the steam release valve to sealed. Select Manual and set the timer for 12 minutes on high.

3. When cooking is complete, quick release the pressure. Unlock and remove the lid.

4. Using a slotted spoon, transfer the ingredients to a blender, along with about 1 cup of the cooking liquid and the cilantro. Purée until smooth. Season with more salt, if necessary.

Troubleshooting tip: If the sauce is too thick, stir in more of the water the tomatoes were cooked in—⅓ cup at a time—until the desired consistency is achieved.

Spicy Salsa Verde

PREP TIME: 5 minutes ✳ MANUAL: 10 minutes on high pressure ✳ RELEASE: Quick
TOTAL TIME: 15 minutes ✳ MAKES: 3 to 4 cups

Salsa verde is a must in your Mexican-food repertoire! It's made with fresh ingredients—like tomatillos, onion, garlic, cilantro, and jalapeño peppers. You'll find that this classic salsa is such a cinch to make in your Instant Pot®, you'll never buy the store-bought stuff again. And there really isn't anything better than homemade salsa. Serve it with chips for dipping while enjoying the big game, or cook a pork roast or chicken breast in the salsa for a tasty taco filling.

2½ pounds tomatillos, husks removed
1 medium onion, roughly chopped
3 garlic cloves, peeled
1 handful cilantro sprigs
4 jalapeño peppers, stemmed
Coarse salt

1. In the Instant Pot®, combine the tomatillos, onion, garlic, cilantro, and jalapeños. Pour in 1½ cups water and season with salt.

2. Lock the lid into place and set the steam release valve to sealed. Select Manual and set the timer for 10 minutes on high.

3. When cooking is complete, quick release the pressure. Unlock and remove the lid.

4. Remove the cilantro sprigs, and transfer the remaining ingredients to a blender, along with about 1 cup of the cooking liquid. Purée until smooth. Season with more salt, if necessary.

Option tip: Take your classic salsa verde to a whole other level by adding 3 to 4 ripe avocados to the blender when puréeing in step 4.

FRIJOLES BORRACHOS, PAGE 32

CHAPTER 3

Rice & Beans

Classic Mexican Rice

PREP TIME: 5 minutes ✳ SAUTÉ: 7 minutes ✳ MANUAL: 10 minutes on high pressure

RELEASE: Quick ✳ TOTAL TIME: 25 minutes ✳ SERVES: 6 to 8

Mexican rice (a.k.a. *sopa de arroz*) is a staple in every Mexican kitchen. My *abuelita* made Mexican rice at least once a week to serve with dinner. And sometimes, I would just eat it as my main meal topped with salsa and shredded cheese. Traditionally, Mexican rice is made on the stove top, but what I love about making this classic family recipe is that I don't have to sacrifice any of the comforting flavor when using the Instant Pot®, and my rice comes out perfect every single time.

3 Roma tomatoes

½ medium white
  onion, peeled

2 garlic cloves, peeled

2 cups chicken broth

2 tablespoons vegetable oil

1 cup long-grain rice

2 cilantro sprigs

1. In a blender, purée the tomatoes, onion, garlic, and chicken broth until smooth. Set aside.

2. Set the Instant Pot® to Sauté and adjust to More for high. Heat the oil in the pot, add the rice, and fry for 5 to 7 minutes, or until golden brown. Carefully pour in the tomato purée and stir gently to combine. Add the cilantro.

3. Lock the lid into place and set the steam release valve to sealed. Select Manual and set the timer for 10 minutes.

4. When cooking is complete, quick release the pressure. Unlock and remove the lid.

5. Remove the cilantro sprigs. Fluff the rice with a fork. Serve.

Substitution tip: Do you prefer the flavor and texture of jasmine rice? Substitute 1 cup jasmine rice for the long-grain rice, and reduce the cooking time to 8 minutes on high.

Arroz Blanco

WHITE RICE

PREP TIME: 5 minutes ✳ SAUTÉ: 3 minutes ✳ MANUAL: 10 minutes on high pressure
RELEASE: Natural ✳ TOTAL TIME: 28 minutes ✳ SERVES: 6 to 8

Not all Mexican rice is red! For example, this white rice is just as much a staple to serve with saucy dishes like Pork Chile Colorado (page 106), Ropa Vieja a la Mexicana (page 109), and leftover Sopa de Lentejas (page 36). But this isn't just some boring rice. This Mexican white rice dish is flavored with onion, garlic, chicken broth, and a couple of sprigs of cilantro. This recipe is sure to be your new go-to for white rice.

½ medium white
   onion, peeled
2 garlic cloves, peeled
2 cups chicken broth
2 tablespoons butter
1 cup long-grain rice
Coarse salt
2 cilantro sprigs

1. In a blender, purée the onion, garlic, and chicken broth until smooth.

2. Set the Instant Pot® to Sauté and adjust to More for high. Heat the butter in the pot until completely melted. Add the rice and sauté for 2 to 3 minutes, or until just opaque. Pour in the onion purée. Season lightly with salt and add the cilantro sprigs.

3. Lock the lid into place and set the steam valve to sealed. Select Manual and set the timer for 10 minutes on high.

4. When cooking is complete, allow the pressure to release naturally. Unlock and remove the lid.

5. Remove the cilantro sprigs. Fluff the rice with a fork. Serve.

Substitution tip: Easily transform your Arroz Blanco into rice pilaf by stirring ⅓ cup dried fideo pasta in with the rice. Then, once the rice has cooked completely, stir in ⅓ cup chopped fresh cilantro and ½ cup chopped pecans or sliced almonds.

Arroz Verde

GREEN RICE

PREP TIME: 5 minutes ✳ SAUTÉ: 3 minutes ✳ MANUAL: 10 minutes on high pressure
RELEASE: Natural ✳ TOTAL TIME: 38 minutes ✳ SERVES: 6 to 8

To round out our trio of rice dishes in the colors of the Mexican flag—red, white, and green—I present you with this flavorful green rice known simply as Arroz Verde. Tomatillos, green chiles, and cilantro are what give this rice its vibrant color and explosive flavor. This rice pairs nicely with roast meats like traditional pork carnitas or *lengua*, but it also makes for a tasty treat for breakfast served with a fried egg, refried beans, and a couple of slices of queso fresco.

5 tomatillos, husks removed
6 to 8 cilantro sprigs
1 poblano pepper, seeded and stemmed
½ medium white onion, cut into large chunks
2 garlic cloves, peeled
2 cups chicken broth
2 tablespoons vegetable oil
1 cup long-grain rice
Coarse salt

1. In a blender, purée the tomatillos, cilantro, poblano,, onion, garlic, and chicken broth until smooth.

2. Set the Instant Pot® to Sauté and adjust to More for high. Heat the vegetable oil in the pot, add the rice, and sauté for 2 to 3 minutes, or until just opaque. Stir in the tomatillo purée. Season lightly with salt.

3. Lock the lid into place and set the steam release valve to sealed. Select Manual and set the timer for 10 minutes on high.

4. When cooking is complete, allow the pressure to release naturally. Unlock and remove the lid.

5. Fluff the rice with a fork. Serve.

Option tip: Save a few minutes in the kitchen by omitting tomatillos, cilantro, poblano, onion, and garlic, and substituting 1¼ cups salsa verde and ¾ cup of chicken broth for the tomatillo purée.

Frijoles de la Olla

COOKED BEANS

PREP TIME: 5 minutes ✳ **MANUAL:** 45 minutes on high pressure ✳ **RELEASE:** Natural
TOTAL TIME: 1 hour 15 minutes ✳ **MAKES:** about 8 cups

Literally translated, *frijoles de la olla* means "beans from the pot." Cooked pinto beans are the base for many a Mexican recipe, but they are also delicious served on their own. My *abuelito* always liked to enjoy a bowl of Frijoles de la Olla fresh from the pot served with chopped onion, crushed Mexican oregano, and warm corn or flour tortillas. With the Instant Pot®, you no longer have to wait for hours to enjoy this comforting soup.

2 pounds dried pinto beans

3 garlic cloves, peeled

2 to 3 teaspoons coarse salt

Chopped white onion,
   for garnish

Dried Mexican oregano,
   crushed, for garnish

Warm corn or flour tortillas,
   for serving (optional)

Sliced queso fresco, for
   serving (optional)

1. Pick through the beans to remove any rocks or debris. Rinse with cold water.

2. In the Instant Pot®, place the beans and garlic. Fill two-thirds full with water.

3. Lock the lid into place and set the steam valve to sealed. Select Manual and set the timer for 45 minutes on high.

4. When cooking is complete, allow the pressure to release naturally. Unlock and remove the lid.

5. Season the beans with the salt to taste.

6. To serve, ladle the beans into bowls and garnish with chopped onion and crushed Mexican oregano. Serve with warm corn or flour tortillas and a couple of slices of queso fresco, if desired. Enjoy!

Freezing tip: Cooked beans are great for freezing and using later in other recipes. Let leftover beans cool completely. Divide into 1½-cup servings and freeze in airtight containers. Let defrost overnight in refrigerator before using.

Frijoles Borrachos
DRUNKEN BEANS

PREP TIME: 10 minutes ✷ SAUTÉ: 9 minutes ✷ MANUAL: 60 minutes on high pressure
RELEASE: Natural ✷ TOTAL TIME: 1 hour 45 minutes ✷ SERVES: 8 to 10

Borracho beans are always a hit when served at potlucks or family gatherings. This boozy take on traditional cowboy beans (a.k.a. *frijoles charros*) gets an added kick of flavor with the addition of ice-cold Mexican beer. And did I mention that there's also bacon in the mix? You can never go wrong with bacon and beer! Like most of the bean recipes in this book, hold off on seasoning with salt until after the beans are cooked, otherwise you'll be left with hard, undercooked beans—or so says an old Mexican wives' tale.

6 slices bacon, cut into
  1-inch strips
½ medium yellow onion,
  finely chopped
3 serrano chiles, finely
  chopped
2 garlic cloves, minced
1 pound dried pinto beans
6 to 8 cilantro sprigs
1 (12-ounce) bottle
  Mexican beer
1½ to 2 teaspoons
  coarse salt

1. Set the Instant Pot® to Sauté and adjust to More for high. Fry the bacon in the pot for 4 to 6 minutes, or until cooked through.

2. Stir in the onion, chiles, and garlic. Sauté for an additional 2 to 3 minutes, or until the onion is translucent.

3. Add the beans, cilantro, beer, and enough water to reach the two-thirds-full mark inside the Instant Pot®.

4. Lock the lid into place and set the steam release valve to sealed. Select Manual and set the timer for 60 minutes on high.

5. When cooking is complete, allow the pressure to release naturally. Unlock and remove the lid.

6. Season the beans with the coarse salt, ladle into bowls, and serve.

Substitution tip: Short on time in the kitchen? Substitute 2 (30-ounce) cans of cooked pinto beans for the dried pinto beans. Reduce the cooking time to 20 minutes on high.

Frijoles Meneados

REFRIED BEANS

PREP TIME: 5 minutes ✻ SAUTÉ: 1 minute ✻ MANUAL: 10 minutes on high pressure
RELEASE: Natural ✻ TOTAL TIME: 45 minutes ✻ SERVES: 8

If you like traditional refried beans, you're going to love Frijoles Meneados! Popular in the Mexican state of Sonora, they are a smoother, creamier version of classic refried beans, with the same delectable flavor. My grandmother made the best Frijoles Meneados I've ever had. The secret to her beans was bacon grease and a splash of milk. I've made Gramm's beans even creamier by adding Mexican crema (or sour cream).

4 cups cooked pinto beans, plus 2 cups cooking liquid

2 cups bean broth

½ cup milk

2 tablespoons bacon grease, lard, or vegetable shortening

1 serrano chile, finely chopped

⅓ cup Mexican crema or sour cream

1 cup shredded Oaxaca or mozzarella cheese

1. In a blender, pulse the beans, bean broth, and milk until smooth.

2. Set the Instant Pot® to Sauté and adjust to More for high. Heat the bacon grease in the pot, add the chile, and sauté for about 30 seconds. Add the bean mixture and Mexican crema, stirring until well combined. Stir in the shredded Oaxaca cheese.

3. Lock the lid into place and set the steam release valve to sealed. Select Manual and set the timer for 10 minutes on high.

4. When cooking is complete, allow the pressure to release naturally. Unlock and remove the lid.

5. Stir the beans gently to combine. Serve immediately.

Substitution tip: Traditionally, *frijoles meneados* are made using cooked pinto beans, but you can use black beans or Peruanos (Peruvian beans) instead

Frijoles Puercos
PORK AND BEAN STEW

PREP TIME: 15 minutes ✳ **SAUTÉ:** 17 minutes ✳ **MANUAL:** 60 minutes on high pressure
RELEASE: Natural ✳ **TOTAL TIME:** 1 hour 55 minutes ✳ **SERVES:** 8 to 10

Frijoles Puercos, a traditional pork and bean soup, is a meat-lover's dream. While this classic bean soup is usually made using cooked beans, I've discovered that in the same amount of time it takes to simmer this soup on the stove, I can make it in my Instant Pot® using dried beans, and get a richer and heartier flavor.

6 slices bacon, cut into 1-inch pieces

4 ounces Mexican pork chorizo, casings removed

2 boneless smoked pork chops, cut into bite-size pieces

4 slices deli ham, chopped

4 pork hot dog franks, cut into 1-inch slices

½ medium white onion, chopped

2 serrano chiles, finely chopped

3 garlic cloves, minced

3 Roma tomatoes, chopped

1 pound dried pinto beans

Handful cilantro sprigs

1 teaspoon crushed dried Mexican oregano

1½ teaspoons coarse salt

Warm tortillas, for serving (optional)

1. Set the Instant Pot® to Sauté and adjust to More for high. Fry the bacon in the pot for 4 to 6 minutes, or until cooked through.

2. Add the chorizo and smoked pork chops; sauté for 3 to 5 minutes, or until cooked through.

3. Add the ham and hot dog franks; sauté for an additional 3 minutes.

4. Stir in the onion, chiles, and garlic. Sauté for 2 to 3 minutes, or just until the onion is translucent.

5. Add the tomatoes, beans, cilantro, oregano, and enough water to reach the two-thirds mark on the inside of the Instant Pot®.

6. Lock the lid into place and set the steam release valve to sealed. Select Manual and set the timer for 60 minutes on high.

7. When cooking is complete, allow the pressure to release naturally. Unlock and remove the lid.

8. Season the beans with the coarse salt, ladle into bowls, and serve with warm tortillas (if desired).

Option tip: Instead of warm tortillas, you can serve this dish with crusty bolillo rolls or any other crusty bread to dip in the rich broth.

Sopa de Garbanzos

CHICKPEA SOUP

PREP TIME: 10 minutes * SAUTÉ: 8 minutes * MANUAL: 40 minutes on high pressure

RELEASE: Natural * TOTAL TIME: 1 hour 25 minutes * SERVES: 6 to 8

This is a Mexican chickpea soup made with smoked pork chops, onion, tomatoes, carrots, fresh jalapeño peppers, and spinach. My version of this classic soup is a combination of the soup I remember from my childhood with pieces of pork and my *suegra*'s recipe, which included sautéing the onion and tomato for the broth. This is a hearty and delicious soup the whole family can enjoy.

2 tablespoons vegetable oil

1 pound boneless smoked pork chops, cut into bite-size pieces

½ medium white onion, thinly sliced

1 jalapeño pepper, seeded and finely chopped

2 garlic cloves, minced

4 medium carrots, peeled and thinly sliced

3 Roma tomatoes, finely chopped

1 pound dried chickpeas

1 teaspoon freshly ground black pepper

1 teaspoon crushed dried Mexican oregano

1½ teaspoons coarse salt

2 cups roughly chopped baby spinach

1. Set the Instant Pot® to Sauté and adjust to More for high. Heat the vegetable oil in the pot, add the pork chops, and sauté for about 5 minutes, or until lightly golden.

2. Add the onion, jalapeño, garlic, and carrots. Sauté for an additional 3 minutes, or until the onion is translucent.

3. Add the tomatoes, chickpeas, and enough water to reach the two-thirds mark inside the Instant Pot®; season with the pepper and oregano.

4. Lock the lid into place and set the steam release valve to sealed. Select Manual and set the timer for 40 minutes on high.

5. When cooking is complete, allow the pressure to release naturally. Unlock and remove the lid.

6. Season the soup with the salt. Stir in the spinach just before serving.

Substitution tip: Need dinner on the table in 30 minutes? Substitute 2 (29-ounce) cans of chickpeas for the dried chickpeas. Reduce the cooking time to 20 minutes on high.

Sopa de Lentejas

LENTIL SOUP

PREP TIME: 10 minutes ✳ SAUTÉ: 8 minutes ✳ MANUAL: 20 minutes on high pressure
RELEASE: Natural ✳ TOTAL TIME: 1 hour ✳ SERVES: 8

Sopa de Lentejas is another of my favorite soups from childhood that I just had to include in this cookbook, because it's perfect for making in the Instant Pot®. Bacon, onion, serrano chiles, garlic, carrots, tomatoes, and cilantro come together to make a flavorful base for this lentil soup. Soups are one of my favorite ways to add more vegetables to our diet, so I always add a couple of cups of chopped fresh spinach just before serving.

6 slices bacon, cut into 1-inch pieces

½ medium white onion, chopped

2 serrano chiles, finely chopped

2 garlic cloves, minced

2 medium carrots, peeled and diced

3 Roma tomatoes, diced

1 pound dried lentils

Handful cilantro sprigs

Coarse salt

2 cups roughly chopped spinach or Swiss chard

1. Set the Instant Pot® to Sauté and adjust to More for high. Fry the bacon in the pot for 4 to 6 minutes, or until cooked through.

2. Add the onion, chiles, garlic, and carrots; sauté for about 3 minutes, or until the onion is translucent.

3. Stir in the tomatoes, lentils, and enough water to reach the two-thirds mark inside the Instant Pot®. Add the cilantro.

4. Lock the lid into place and set the steam release valve to sealed. Select Manual and set the timer for 20 minutes on high.

5. When cooking is complete, allow the pressure to release naturally. Unlock and remove the lid.

6. Season the lentil soup with salt to taste. Stir in the spinach just before serving.

Substitution tip: Make this soup completely vegetarian by omitting the bacon and sautéing the onion, chiles, garlic, and carrots in 1 tablespoon of vegetable oil.

"Soups are one of my favorite ways to add more vegetables to our diet . . ."

GREEN CHICKEN POZOLE, PAGE 52

CHAPTER 4

Soups, Stews & Chilies

Albóndigas en Caldillo
MEATBALL SOUP IN TOMATO BROTH

PREP TIME: 10 minutes ✳ MANUAL: 20 minutes on high pressure ✳ RELEASE: Quick
TOTAL TIME: 30 minutes ✳ SERVES: 6

If you're not familiar with Albóndigas en Caldillo you have been missing out! It is a hearty Mexican meatball soup with veggies, simmered in either a tomato-based broth (as here) or a clear broth. This is my go-to soup when I'm craving some good old-fashioned Mexican comfort food like my *abuelitos* (grandparents) used to make. I'm an Instant Pot® convert when it comes to making this classic Mexican soup, because it results in fluffier meatballs and a more flavorful dish.

For the meatballs

½ pound ground beef
½ pound ground pork
2 tablespoons long-grain rice
2 tablespoons plain dry
  bread crumbs
2 tablespoons
  old-fashioned oats
1 large egg
1 large Roma tomato,
  finely chopped
¼ medium white onion,
  finely chopped
1 serrano chile, finely
  chopped (optional)
1 garlic clove, minced
¾ teaspoon coarse salt
¼ teaspoon freshly ground
  black pepper
¼ teaspoon crushed dried
  Mexican oregano

For the soup

2 cups Caldillo de Jitomate
  (page 16) or tomato sauce
3 medium carrots, peeled
  and thinly sliced
2 medium Yukon Gold
  potatoes, peeled and diced
2 medium Mexican
  calabacitas or zucchini, cut
  into bite-size pieces
4 cilantro sprigs
½ teaspoon coarse salt,
  plus more for seasoning
  (optional)
¼ teaspoon freshly ground
  black pepper
¼ teaspoon crushed dried
  Mexican oregano
Chopped fresh cilantro,
  for garnish
Freshly squeezed lime juice,
  for garnish
Warm corn tortillas (optional)

To make the meatballs

> In a large bowl, combine the beef, pork, rice, bread crumbs, oats, egg, tomato, onion, chile, garlic, salt, pepper, and oregano, mixing until the mixture comes together. Divide and shape into 1½- to 2-inch meatballs.

To make the soup

1. Set the Instant Pot® to Sauté and adjust to More for high. Pour in 5 cups water and the tomato sauce. Add the carrots, potatoes, *calabacitas*, and cilantro sprigs. Carefully drop the meatballs, one at a time, into the broth. (Do not stir beyond this point!) Season the broth with the salt, black pepper, and oregano.

2. Lock the lid into place and set the steam release valve to sealed. Select Manual and set the timer for 20 minutes on high.

3. When cooking is complete, quick release the pressure. Unlock and remove the lid.

4. Season with additional salt, if necessary. Ladle the soup into bowls. Garnish with chopped cilantro and a squeeze of fresh lime juice. Serve with warm corn tortillas (if desired).

Option tip: To make the traditional *albóndigas* soup in a clear broth, omit the Caldillo de Jitomate and increase the water to 7 cups.

Black Bean, Sweet Potato, and Chorizo Chili

PREP TIME: 10 minutes ✷ **SAUTÉ:** 10 minutes ✷ **MANUAL:** 60 minutes on high pressure
RELEASE: Natural ✷ **TOTAL TIME:** 1 hour 45 minutes ✷ **SERVES:** 8

One of my favorite Tex-Mex-inspired flavor combinations is black beans, sweet potatoes, and spicy Mexican chorizo! The flavor combination works perfectly in just about anything from simple quesadillas to this thick and hearty chili seasoned with chipotle powder, oregano, cumin, onion, garlic, green bell peppers, and a dark Mexican beer. My not-so-secret ingredient for a rich chili with subtle hints that remind you of a classic mole? Mexican chocolate! One tablet is all you need to bring this fiery chili together.

1 tablespoon vegetable oil
1 pound Mexican
    pork chorizo
2 green bell peppers, diced
1 large white onion, diced
4 garlic cloves, minced
2 medium sweet potatoes,
    peeled and diced
3 Roma tomatoes, diced
1 pound dried black beans
1 (12-ounce) bottle dark
    Mexican beer (I use
    Negra Modelo)
1 (3-ounce) tablet Mexican
    chocolate, cut into eighths

1½ tablespoons chipotle
    chile powder
1 teaspoon crushed dried
    Mexican oregano
½ teaspoon ground cumin
½ teaspoon freshly ground
    black pepper
1 to 1½ teaspoons
    coarse salt
Sour cream, for garnish
Crumbled queso cotija,
    for garnish

1. Set the Instant Pot® to Sauté and adjust to More for high. Heat the vegetable oil in the pot, add the chorizo, and sauté for 5 to 7 minutes, or until cooked through.

2. Add the bell peppers, onion, and garlic; sauté for 2 to 3 minutes, or until the onion is translucent. Stir in the sweet potatoes, tomatoes, and black beans.

3. Pour in 6 cups water and the beer; season with the Mexican chocolate, chipotle powder, oregano, cumin, and pepper.

4. Lock the lid into place and set the steam release valve to sealed. Select Manual and set the timer for 60 minutes on high.

5. When cooking is complete, allow the pressure to release naturally. Unlock and remove the lid.

6. Season the chili with the salt and ladle into bowls. Garnish with a dollop of sour cream and crumbled queso cotija.

Option tip: Like your chili even thicker? In a small bowl, dissolve 3 tablespoons of masa harina in ½ cup water. Stir into the chili as soon as you remove the lid in step 5. Set the Instant Pot® to Sauté and let the chili simmer, uncovered, for 3 to 5 minutes, or until it starts to thicken.

Caldo de Pollo

MEXICAN CHICKEN SOUP

PREP TIME: 10 minutes ✶ MANUAL: 20 minutes on high pressure ✶ RELEASE: Natural
TOTAL TIME: 50 minutes ✶ SERVES: 6

When thinking of my favorite Mexican soups to include in this chapter, Caldo de Pollo was at the top of the list. My *abuelita* made this Mexican chicken soup once a week, because there is nothing a hot, warm bowl of chicken soup can't cure. The common cold, the flu, heartbreak, a bad day . . . Caldo de Pollo is sure to make it all better! The thing that makes this classic soup distinctly Mexican is how it is served garnished with a tablespoon of your favorite salsa, a squeeze of fresh lime juice, and plenty of warm tortillas.

2¼ pounds boneless, skinless chicken breast or thighs, cut into large chunks

1 medium onion, roughly chopped

3 whole garlic cloves, peeled

1 serrano chile, stem removed and split in half lengthwise

6 cilantro sprigs

2 dried bay leaves

1½ teaspoons coarse salt

½ teaspoon freshly ground black pepper

½ teaspoon crushed dried Mexican oregano

2 ears corn, husks removed and cut into 2-inch pieces

2 celery stalks, cut into large chunks

4 medium carrots, peeled and cut into large chunks

1 cup green beans, trimmed

3 medium Yukon Gold potatoes, peeled and cut into quarters

2 medium Mexican *calabacitas* or zucchini, cut into large chunks

Salsa, for serving

Freshly squeezed lime juice, for serving

Warm corn or flour tortillas, for serving (optional)

1. In the Instant Pot®, combine the chicken, onion, garlic, chile, cilantro, bay leaves, salt, pepper, and oregano. Top with the corn pieces, celery, carrots, green beans, potatoes, and *calabacitas*. Pour in enough water to reach the two-thirds mark inside the Instant Pot®.

2. Lock the lid into place and set the steam release valve to sealed. Select Manual and set the timer for 20 minutes on high.

3. When cooking is complete, allow the pressure to release naturally. Unlock and remove the lid. Remove and discard the bay leaves.

4. Ladle the soup into bowls. Serve with your favorite salsa, a squeeze of fresh lime juice, and warm corn or flour tortillas (if desired).

Technique tip: How to eat tortillas with soup like a pro: Place a warm tortilla in the palm of your hand. With your other hand slowly roll the tortilla up tightly like a taquito and dip the tortilla into the broth. Repeat as necessary.

Sopa de Fideo
MEXICAN NOODLE SOUP

PREP TIME: 5 minutes ✳ SAUTÉ: 6 minutes ✳ MANUAL: 6 minutes on high pressure
RELEASE: Quick ✳ TOTAL TIME: 20 minutes ✳ SERVES: 6 to 8

For those of us who grew up in Mexican households, Sopa de Fideo is one of those classic comfort foods that will always bring to mind fond memories of our childhood. My *abuelito* always made this simple Mexican noodle soup on rainy days and whenever I was sick. Simmered in a light tomato broth seasoned with onion and fresh cilantro, Sopa de Fideo is a comforting soup both grown-ups and kids will love.

3 Roma tomatoes
½ medium white onion
2 tablespoons vegetable oil
8 ounces fideo pasta
2 cups chicken broth
Coarse salt
3 cilantro sprigs

1. In a blender, puree the tomatoes, onion, and 3 cups of water until smooth.

2. Set the Instant Pot® to Sauté and adjust to More for high. Heat the vegetable oil in the pot, add the pasta, and sauté for 4 to 6 minutes, or until golden brown. Carefully pour in the tomato purée and chicken broth; season lightly with coarse salt. Add the cilantro.

3. Lock the lid into place and set the steam release valve to sealed. Select Manual and set the timer for 6 minutes on high.

4. When cooking is complete, allow the pressure to release naturally. Serve the soup immediately.

Substitution tip: Sopa de Fideo can be made with any shape of pasta. Some of my childhood favorites include alphabet pasta, stars, and small shells.

Tex-Mex Chili

PREP TIME: 10 minutes ✳ SAUTÉ: 11 minutes ✳ MANUAL: 20 minutes on high pressure
RELEASE: Natural ✳ TOTAL TIME: 55 minutes ✳ SERVES: 8 to 10

You can't have a chapter titled Soups, Stews & Chilies without a classic Tex-Mex chili recipe. I didn't start to make chili on my own, completely from scratch, until I got married. Up until then, most of the chili con carne I grew up eating came from a can. The canned stuff doesn't even come close to the real thing! My version is thick and hearty, made with ground beef and beans in a rich, flavorful sauce seasoned with a variety of herbs and spices.

1 tablespoon vegetable oil
2¼ pounds ground beef
1 medium white
   onion, chopped
2 serrano chiles,
   finely chopped
2 Roasted Poblano Peppers
   (page 134), peeled, seeded,
   and cut into thin strips
4 garlic cloves, minced
4 Roma tomatoes, chopped
1 (15.5-ounce) can black
   beans, drained
1 (15.5-ounce) can pinto
   beans, drained
1 tablespoon ancho
   chile powder
1 tablespoon California
   chile powder

1½ teaspoons coarse salt,
   plus more for seasoning
   (optional)
1 teaspoon paprika
1 teaspoon ground cumin
1 teaspoon crushed dried
   Mexican oregano
½ teaspoon freshly ground
   black pepper
1 cup beef broth
6 to 8 cilantro sprigs
3 tablespoons masa harina
Sour cream, for garnish
Chopped tomato, for garnish
Chopped onion, for garnish
Chopped fresh cilantro,
   for garnish
Crumbled queso cotija,
   for garnish

> CONTINUED

Tex-Mex Chili

> CONTINUED

1. Set the Instant Pot® to Sauté and adjust to More for high. Heat the vegetable oil in the pot, add the ground beef, and sauté for 6 to 8 minutes, breaking it up with the back of a wooden spoon, until no longer pink. Add the onion, chiles, roasted pepper strips, and garlic. Sauté for an additional 2 to 3 minutes, or until the onion is translucent.

2. Stir in the tomatoes, black beans, and pinto beans. Season with the chile powders, salt, paprika, cumin, oregano, and pepper. Pour in 2 cups of water and the beef broth. Add the cilantro sprigs.

3. Lock the lid into place and set the steam release valve to sealed. Select Manual and set the timer for 20 minutes on high.

4. When cooking is complete, allow the pressure to release naturally. Unlock and remove the lid.

5. In a small bowl, dissolve the masa harina in ½ cup of water; immediately stir into the hot chili. Season the chili with more salt, if desired.

6. Ladle the chili into bowls. Garnish with a dollop of sour cream and chopped tomato, onion, and cilantro. Sprinkle a little crumbled queso cotija on top. Serve with Masa Harina Cornbread (page 133).

Option tip: Serve leftovers of this mouthwatering chili atop nachos, French fries, or bacon-wrapped hot dogs.

Cocido de Res

MEXICAN BEEF SOUP

PREP TIME: 10 minutes   ✳   MANUAL: 60 minutes on high pressure   ✳   RELEASE: Natural

TOTAL TIME: 1 hour 30 minutes   ✳   SERVES: 8

This classic Mexican beef and vegetable soup goes by many names, including *cocido, puchero,* and Caldo de Res. I'm sure you'll just call it delicious! Traditionally, this soup simmers on the stove for hours, until the beef stew meat and corn are tender, but with the Instant Pot® you only need to let this soup simmer for one hour. In my family, we like to serve it with Classic Mexican Rice (page 28), Nopales (page 136), a squeeze of fresh lime juice, a heaping tablespoon full of Classic Tomatillo and Árbol Chile Salsa (page 18), and plenty of warm corn tortillas.

3½ pounds beef stew meat

2 ears corn, each cut into 3 pieces

1 medium white onion, halved

3 whole garlic cloves, peeled

6 cilantro sprigs

1½ teaspoons coarse salt

½ teaspoon freshly ground black pepper

4 medium carrots, peeled and cut into bite-size pieces

1 cup green beans, cut into 1-inch pieces

3 medium Yukon Gold potatoes, cut into eighths

2 medium chayote squash, peeled, pitted, and cut into eighths

¼ head cabbage, roughly chopped

Freshly squeezed lime juice, for garnish

Salsa, for garnish

Warm corn tortillas, for serving (optional)

> CONTINUED

Cocido de Res

> CONTINUED

1. In the Instant Pot®, combine the beef, corn, onion, garlic, and cilantro. Season with the salt and pepper.

2. Add the carrots, green beans, potatoes, chayote squash, and cabbage. Fill the Instant Pot® with enough water to reach the two-thirds mark.

3. Lock the lid into place and set the steam release valve to sealed. Select Manual and set the timer for 60 minutes on high.

4. When cooking is complete, allow the pressure to release naturally. Unlock and remove the lid.

5. Ladle the soup into bowls. Garnish with a squeeze of fresh lime juice and your favorite salsa. Serve with warm corn tortillas (if desired).

Option tip: Add a splash of vibrant color to this soup by pouring in 1 cup of Salsa de Chile Colorado (page 21) or red enchilada sauce with the water for a soup called *cocido rojo.*

Gallina Pinta

BEEF, BEAN, AND HOMINY SOUP

PREP TIME: 10 minutes ✱ **SAUTÉ:** 11 minutes ✱ **MANUAL:** 60 minutes on high pressure
RELEASE: Natural ✱ **TOTAL TIME:** 1 hour 15 minutes ✱ **SERVES:** 6 to 8

Gallina Pinta is a traditional soup popular in the state of Sonora, where my maternal grandmother was raised. How this Mexican beef soup got the name Gallina Pinta, which translates to "spotted hen," I do not know—there is no chicken in it whatsoever—but it's been one of my favorites since childhood. This beef, bean, and hominy soup is perfect for cooking in the Instant Pot®, because instead of waiting for hours for the beans and meat to soften, this soup cooks for only an hour!

1 tablespoon vegetable oil
2¼ pounds oxtails
½ medium white onion, diced
3 Hungarian wax peppers, thinly sliced
2 whole garlic cloves, peeled
2 cups dried pinto beans
1 (29-ounce) can white hominy, drained
1 dried bay leaf
1 teaspoon crushed dried Mexican oregano
Coarse salt
Chopped red onion, for garnish
Chopped fresh cilantro, for garnish
Freshly squeezed lime juice, for garnish
Warm flour tortillas, for serving (optional)

1. Set the Instant Pot® to Sauté and adjust to More for high. Heat the vegetable oil in the pot, add the oxtails, and sauté for 6 to 8 minutes, flipping once, until lightly browned on both sides.

2. Stir in the onion, peppers, and garlic. Sauté for 2 to 3 minutes, or until the onion is translucent.

3. Add the pinto beans, hominy, bay leaf, oregano, and 6 cups of water.

4. Lock the lid into place and set the steam release valve to sealed. Select Manual and set the timer for 60 minutes on high.

5. When cooking is complete, allow the pressure to release naturally. Season the soup with salt. Remove and discard the bay leaf.

6. To serve, ladle the soup into bowls. Garnish with chopped red onion, cilantro, and a squeeze of fresh lime juice. Serve with warm flour tortillas (if desired).

Substitution tip: This soup is traditionally made with oxtails, but because they're not always easy to find, beef shanks will also work well.

Green Chicken Pozole

PREP TIME: 5 minutes ✳ MANUAL: 20 minutes on high pressure ✳ RELEASE: Natural
TOTAL TIME: 50 minutes ✳ SERVES: 8

Pozole *verde* is a traditional Mexican soup that can be made with either chicken or pork in a salsa verde broth. The broth gets its vibrant green color from my homemade Spicy Salsa Verde (page 24), made with fresh tomatillos and green chiles. And just like with traditional pozole, the garnishes—finely shredded cabbage or lettuce, chopped onion, sliced radishes, and a squeeze of fresh lime juice—play just as important a role as the chicken and hominy.

3 pounds boneless chicken breasts or thighs, cut into large chunks

1 medium onion, halved

3 garlic cloves, minced

4 cilantro sprigs

1 (29-ounce) can white hominy, drained

3 cups Spicy Salsa Verde (page 24)

2 cups chicken broth

½ teaspoon coarse salt, plus more for seasoning (optional)

½ teaspoon crushed dried Mexican oregano

Chopped red onion, for garnish

Shredded cabbage or lettuce, for garnish

Sliced radishes, for garnish

Freshly squeezed lime juice, for garnish

Tostada shells or tortilla chips, for serving (optional)

1. In the Instant Pot®, combine the chicken, onion, garlic, cilantro, hominy, and salsa verde. Add the chicken broth, salt, oregano, and 3 cups water.

2. Lock the lid into place and set the steam release valve to sealed. Select Manual and set the timer for 20 minutes on high.

3. When cooking is complete, allow the pressure to release naturally. Unlock and remove the lid.

4. Season the pozole with more salt, if necessary. Ladle into bowls and garnish with chopped onion, shredded cabbage, sliced radishes, and a squeeze of fresh lime juice. Serve with tostada shells or tortilla chips (if desired).

Substitution tip: Haven't tried making the Spicy Salsa Verde yet? Substitute 1 (28-ounce) can green enchilada sauce. Also, if you prefer more hominy in your pozole, add 1 (15-ounce) can.

Menudo/Pancita

TRIPE SOUP

PREP TIME: 5 minutes ✳ **MANUAL:** 1 hour 15 minutes on high pressure
RELEASE: Natural ✳ **TOTAL TIME:** 1 hour 45 minutes ✳ **SERVES:** 8

Growing up, Sundays meant Menudo (or what my *abuelito* called *Pancita*), whether it was the stuff from the can or Pappy's homemade. I've been hesitant to share my menudo recipe up until now because it can be a long process of cooking the tripe on the stove for hours until tender. But the Instant Pot® has changed all that. Menudo is one of those dishes that can vary from region to region or family to family. My recipe is inspired by Jalisco-style menudo, which consists of just the beef tripe simmered in a red chile broth, which is then garnished with chopped white onion, crushed dried Mexican oregano, and toasted árbol chile flakes for added heat.

1 pound blanket/flat tripe, cut into 2- to 3-inch pieces

1 pound honeycomb tripe, cut into 2- to 3-inch pieces

1 pound book tripe, cut into 2- to 3-inch pieces

1½ cups Salsa de Chile Colorado (page 21) or red enchilada sauce

1½ teaspoons coarse salt, plus more for seasoning (optional)

Chopped white onion, for garnish

Crushed dried Mexican oregano, for garnish

Red pepper flakes or árbol chile flakes, for garnish

Freshly squeezed lime juice, for garnish

Warm corn tortillas, for serving (optional)

1. In the Instant Pot®, combine all of the tripe, the chile sauce, salt, and 6 cups water.

2. Lock the lid into place and set the steam release valve to sealed. Select Manual and set the timer for 1 hour, 15 minutes on high.

3. When cooking is complete, allow the pressure to release naturally. Unlock and remove the lid.

4. Stir the menudo gently to combine; season with additional salt, if desired. Ladle into bowls and garnish with a heaping tablespoon of chopped onion, a pinch of dried Mexican oregano, a dash of red pepper flakes, and a squeeze of fresh lime juice. Serve with warm corn tortillas (if desired).

Option tip: For menudo with hominy, add 1 (29-ounce) can of drained white hominy, 1 teaspoon dried Mexican oregano, and ½ teaspoon ground cumin in with the tripe.

Mole de Olla

SPICY CHICKEN AND VEGETABLE SOUP

PREP TIME: 10 minutes ✳ MANUAL: 20 minutes on high pressure ✳ RELEASE: Quick
TOTAL TIME: 30 minutes ✳ SERVES: 6

Because you can never have too many recipes for chicken soup! Mole de Olla, not to be confused with traditional *mole* sauce, is a classic Mexican soup with a rich dried-chile broth. Traditionally, this soup is made with beef, but my *abuelitos* always made it with chicken. Chock-full of fresh vegetables like corn, carrots, green beans, zucchini, and cabbage, Mole de Olla is a spicy twist on comforting Caldo de Pollo (chicken soup; page 44) that I guarantee will soon become a family favorite.

2 ears corn, husks removed and each ear cut into three pieces

2¼ pounds boneless chicken breasts or thighs, cut into large chunks

1 medium onion, quartered

2 whole garlic cloves, peeled

5 cilantro sprigs

3 medium carrots, peeled and cut into bite-size pieces

1 cup green beans, cut into bite-size pieces

2 medium potatoes, peeled and cut into large chunks

¼ head cabbage, cut into large chunks

2 medium zucchini, cut into large chunks

1½ cups Salsa de Chile Colorado (page 21) or enchilada sauce

2 teaspoons chicken bouillon

1 teaspoon coarse salt, plus more for seasoning (optional)

1 teaspoon crushed dried Mexican oregano

½ teaspoon ground cumin

½ teaspoon freshly ground black pepper

Freshly squeezed lime juice, for garnish

Warm corn tortillas, for serving (optional)

1. In the Instant Pot®, combine the corn, chicken, onion, garlic, cilantro, carrots, green beans, potatoes, cabbage, and zucchini.

2. Pour in the chile sauce and enough water to fill to the two-thirds mark into the Instant Pot®. Add the chicken bouillon, salt, oregano, cumin, and pepper.

3. Lock the lid into place and set the steam release valve to sealed. Select Manual and set the timer for 20 minutes on high.

4. When cooking is complete, quick release the pressure. Unlock and remove the lid. Season the soup with more salt, if necessary.

5. Ladle the soup into bowls. Top with a squeeze of fresh lime juice. Serve with warm corn tortillas (if desired).

Substitution tip: To make traditional Mole de Olla with beef, substitute 2¼ pounds of beef stew meat for the chicken and increase the cook time to 40 minutes on high.

Pozole Blanco

WHITE POZOLE

PREP TIME: 5 minutes ✳ MANUAL: 55 minutes on high pressure ✳ RELEASE: Natural

TOTAL TIME: 1 hour 30 minutes ✳ SERVES: 8

Pozole Blanco is pozole in its simplest form. In this toned-down version of pozole, the flavors of the pork and hominy shine through and speak for themselves. The subtle flavor of the Hungarian wax peppers adds a hint of spice to this classic soup without overpowering the other flavors. Pozole Blanco is served with all the traditional pozole garnishes—shredded cabbage or lettuce, chopped onion, sliced radishes, and a squeeze of lime juice—but you can also add diced avocado and chopped cilantro.

3½ pounds pork stew meat

3 (15-ounce) cans white hominy, drained

2 Hungarian wax peppers, seeded and thinly sliced

1 medium white onion, thinly sliced

5 garlic cloves, minced

6 cilantro sprigs

2 dried bay leaves

1½ teaspoons coarse salt

1 teaspoon dried Mexican oregano

½ teaspoon freshly ground black pepper

Chopped red onion, for garnish

Shredded cabbage or lettuce, for garnish

Sliced radishes, for garnish

Lime wedges, for garnish

Salsa de Pepino (Cucumber Salsa; page 138), for garnish (optional)

1. In the Instant Pot®, combine the pork, hominy, wax peppers, onion, garlic, and cilantro. Add the bay leaves, salt, oregano, and pepper. Pour in enough water to reach the two-thirds mark inside the pot.

2. Lock the lid into place and set the steam release valve to sealed. Select Manual and set the timer for 55 minutes on high.

3. When cooking is complete, allow the pressure to release naturally. Unlock and remove the lid. Remove and discard the bay leaves.

4. Season the pozole with more salt, if desired. Ladle into bowls and garnish with red onion, cabbage, radishes, lime wedges, and salsa (if desired).

Serving tip: Pozole isn't just for lunch or dinner. It also makes for a hearty breakfast and is believed to be a great hangover cure.

Traditional Red Pork Pozole

PREP TIME: 10 minutes ✳ MANUAL: 60 minutes on high pressure ✳ RELEASE: Natural

TOTAL TIME: 1 hour 35 minutes ✳ SERVES: 6 to 8

Pozole is a popular dish in Mexico. In this chapter alone, you'll find three different versions: Green Chicken Pozole (page 52), Pozole Blanco (page 56), and this one. Pozole is often reserved for special occasions such as birthdays, christenings, first communions, and the holiday season. While it can be made with beef, chicken, or pork, the most popular version of the traditional Mexican soup is red pork pozole, made with tender pieces of boneless pork leg simmered in a red chile broth with hominy.

3 pounds boneless pork leg, cut into 2-inch pieces

3 (15-ounce) cans white hominy, drained

1 medium white onion, halved

3 garlic cloves, minced

Handful cilantro sprigs

2 cups Salsa de Chile Colorado (page 21) or red enchilada sauce

2 dried bay leaves

1½ teaspoons coarse salt

1 teaspoon crushed dried Mexican oregano

¼ teaspoon freshly ground black pepper

Freshly squeezed lime juice, for garnish

Shredded cabbage, for garnish

Chopped onion, for garnish

Sliced radishes, for garnish

Salsa de Pepino (Cucumber Salsa; page 138) or your favorite bottled hot sauce, for garnish

Tostada shells, for serving (optional)

> CONTINUED

Traditional Red Pork Pozole

> CONTINUED

1. In the Instant Pot®, combine the pork, hominy, onion, garlic, and cilantro. Add the chile sauce, bay leaves, salt, oregano, and pepper.

2. Pour in enough water to reach the two-thirds mark inside the Instant Pot®.

3. Lock the lid into place and set the steam release valve to sealed. Select Manual and set the timer for 60 minutes on high.

4. When cooking is complete, allow the pressure to release naturally. Unlock and remove the lid. Remove and discard the bay leaves.

5. Stir the pozole gently to combine. Season with additional salt, if desired. Ladle into bowls. Garnish with a squeeze of fresh lime juice, cabbage, onion, radishes, and a heaping tablespoon of cucumber salsa. Serve with tostada shells (if desired).

Serving tip: Have all the garnishes set out on the table and let your family or guests serve themselves. Be sure to have plenty of crunchy tostada shells on the side.

Vegetarian Chili

PREP TIME: 10 minutes ✳ SAUTÉ: 3 minutes ✳ MANUAL: 20 minutes on high pressure

RELEASE: Natural ✳ TOTAL TIME: 1 hour ✳ SERVES: 8

Who says a hearty chili can't be meatless? This loaded Vegetarian Chili has everything but the kitchen sink: lentils, black beans, corn, onion, tomatoes, garlic, *calabacitas*, carrots, and celery. But wait, there's more! This robust chili is also full of flavor thanks to the Mexican beer, Hungarian wax peppers, cilantro, ancho chile powder, oregano, cumin, and masa harina.

2 tablespoons extra-virgin olive oil

1 medium white onion, chopped

3 garlic cloves, minced

3 Hungarian wax peppers, seeded and finely chopped

3 medium carrots, peeled and chopped

2 celery stalks, chopped

3 Roma tomatoes, seeded and chopped

2 medium Mexican *calabacitas* or zucchini, chopped

1 yellow squash, chopped

1 pound dried lentils

1 (15-ounce) can black beans, drained

1 (15.5-ounce) can golden corn kernels, drained

5 cilantro sprigs

1 (12-ounce) bottle Mexican beer

2 dried bay leaves

2 tablespoons ancho chile powder

1 teaspoon crushed dried Mexican oregano

1 teaspoon ground cumin

½ teaspoon freshly ground black pepper

3 tablespoons masa harina

1 to 1½ teaspoons coarse salt

Mexican crema or sour cream, for garnish

Shredded Colby Jack cheese, for garnish

Chopped red onion, for garnish

Finely chopped fresh cilantro, for garnish

> CONTINUED

Vegetarian Chili

> CONTINUED

1. Set the Instant Pot® to Sauté and adjust to More for high. Heat the olive oil in the pot, add the onion, garlic, and wax peppers, and sauté for 2 to 3 minutes, or until the onion is translucent.

2. Stir in the carrots, celery, tomatoes, *calabacitas*, squash, lentils, black beans, corn, and cilantro. Add the beer and 6 cups of water. Add the bay leaves, ancho chile powder, oregano, cumin, and pepper.

3. Lock the lid into place and set the steam release valve to sealed. Select Manual and set the timer for 20 minutes on high.

4. When cooking is complete, allow the pressure to release naturally. Unlock and remove the lid. Remove and discard the bay leaves.

5. In a small bowl, dissolve the masa harina in ¼ cup of water; stir into the chili. Season the chili with the salt. Lightly mash some of the lentils to help thicken the chili.

6. Ladle the chili into bowls. Garnish with a dollop of Mexican crema, shredded Colby Jack cheese, chopped red onion, and cilantro.

Option tip: Serve this hearty vegetarian chili with warm tortillas, tortilla chips, or Masa Harina Cornbread (page 133).

Chile Relleno Chowder

PREP TIME: 5 minutes ✳ SAUTÉ: 3 minutes ✳ MANUAL: 12 minutes on high pressure

RELEASE: Quick ✳ TOTAL TIME: 20 minutes ✳ SERVES: 6

This flavorful soup was inspired by two of my favorite poblano pepper recipes: *rajas con crema* and *chiles rellenos*. Here, roasted poblano pepper strips, corn, potatoes, and queso fresco swim in a creamy broth. Poblano peppers aren't known for their heat, but they do add a ton of flavor to whatever dish they're used in. Once this soup is served, I like to top it with shredded Colby Jack cheese for even more cheesy goodness.

2 tablespoons butter

½ medium white onion, roughly chopped

2 garlic cloves, minced

8 Roasted Poblano Peppers (page 134), peeled, seeded, and cut into thin strips

4 medium Yukon Gold potatoes, peeled and chopped

1 (15.5-ounce) can golden corn kernels, drained

3 cups vegetable or chicken broth

2½ cups milk, divided

1 cup Mexican crema or sour cream

1 teaspoon coarse salt

½ teaspoon freshly ground black pepper

3 tablespoons cornstarch

10 ounces queso fresco, cut into bite-size cubes

1½ cups shredded Colby Jack cheese

1. Set the Instant Pot® to Sauté and adjust to More for high. Heat the butter in the pot until completely melted, add the onion and garlic, and sauté for 2 to 3 minutes, or until the onion is translucent.

2. Add the roasted poblano strips, potatoes, and corn.

3. Pour in the chicken broth, 2 cups of milk, and the Mexican crema. Season with the salt and pepper.

4. Lock the lid into place and set the steam release valve to sealed. Select Manual and set the timer for 12 minutes on high.

5. When cooking is complete, allow the pressure to release naturally. Unlock and remove the lid.

6. In a small bowl, stir the cornstarch into the remaining ½ cup of milk until completely dissolved. Stir into the hot soup immediately. Mash some of the potatoes lightly with a potato masher or the back of a spoon to help thicken the soup. Stir in the queso fresco.

7. Ladle the soup into bowls. Top each bowl with ¼ cup shredded Colby Jack cheese.

Option tip: For a heartier soup, add 2 boneless, skinless chicken breasts (cut into bite-size pieces) with the poblano pepper strips. Increase the cook time to 15 minutes on high.

CAULIFLOWER TINGA, PAGE 65

CHAPTER 5

Vegetable Mains

Tacos de Rajas con Crema

ROASTED POBLANO STRIPS WITH CREAM TACOS

PREP TIME: 8 minutes ✳ SAUTÉ: 3 minutes ✳ MANUAL: 8 minutes on high pressure
RELEASE: Quick ✳ TOTAL TIME: 20 minutes ✳ SERVES: 6 to 8

Anytime a recipe mentions the word *rajas*, it's referring to Roasted Poblano Peppers (page 134). Anytime you see the words *rajas con crema*, just know that you are in for a delicious treat that consists of roasted poblano pepper strips swimming in Mexican crema that makes for an amazingly delicious meatless taco filling perfect for any night of the week. And best of all, if you roast the poblano peppers ahead of time, you can have dinner on the table in 30 minutes.

2 tablespoons vegetable oil

1 medium white onion, thinly sliced

2 garlic cloves, minced

8 Roasted Poblano Peppers (page 134), peeled, seeded, and cut into thin strips

2 Roma tomatoes, seeded and thinly sliced

1 cup Mexican crema or sour cream

¼ cup whole milk

2 medium Yukon Gold potatoes, peeled and diced

1 (15.25-ounce) can golden corn kernels, drained

Coarse salt

Freshly ground black pepper

Corn tortillas, for serving

Crumbled queso cotija, for garnish

1. Set the Instant Pot® to Sauté and adjust to More for high. Heat the vegetable oil in the pot, add the onion and garlic, and sauté for 2 to 3 minutes, or until the onion is translucent.

2. Stir in the roasted poblano pepper strips, tomatoes, Mexican crema, milk, potatoes, and corn. Season with salt and pepper.

3. Lock the lid into place and set the steam release valve to sealed. Select Manual and set the timer for 8 minutes on high.

4. When cooking is complete, quick release the pressure. Unlock and remove the lid.

5. Stir gently to combine. Heat the corn tortillas on a comal or griddle until soft and pliable. Stack two warm corn tortillas for each taco. Spoon a couple of heaping tablespoons of *rajas con crema* down the center of each tortilla stack. Top with crumbled queso cotija.

Option tip: For a Mexican pasta night, ladle *rajas con crema* over cooked spaghetti. Serve with a green salad and garlic bread.

Cauliflower Tinga

PREP TIME: 5 minutes ✳ SAUTÉ: 3 minutes ✳ MANUAL: 10 minutes on high pressure
RELEASE: Quick ✳ TOTAL TIME: 20 minutes ✳ SERVES: 6 to 8

Going meatless has never been easier with something as tasty as this Cauliflower Tinga. Tender pieces of cauliflower braised in a simple tomato-chipotle sauce can be served as a meatless filling for tacos, tostadas, burritos, or even enchiladas, but it also makes for a delicious side dish loaded with spicy flavor. For a quick and easy meatless meal, serve it atop warm corn tortillas and garnish with pickled onions and chopped cilantro.

4 Roma tomatoes
2 to 4 chipotle chiles in
   adobo sauce
1 tablespoon vegetable oil
1 medium onion, diced
2 garlic cloves, minced
1 head cauliflower,
   roughly chopped
Coarse salt
Freshly ground black pepper
Corn tortillas, for serving
Pickled Red Onions
   (page 139), for garnish
Chopped fresh cilantro,
   for garnish

1. In a blender, purée the tomatoes, chipotle chiles, and 1 cup water until smooth.

2. Set the Instant Pot® to Sauté and adjust to More for high. Heat the vegetable oil in the pot, add the onion and garlic, and sauté for 2 to 3 minutes, or until the onion is translucent.

3. Stir in the cauliflower and tomato-chipotle purée. Season with salt and pepper.

4. Lock the lid into place and set the steam release valve to sealed. Select Manual and set the timer for 10 minutes on high.

5. When cooking is complete, quick release the pressure. Unlock and remove the lid.

6. Spoon the Cauliflower *Tinga* onto corn tortillas. Garnish with pickled red onions and chopped cilantro.

Option tip: Canned chipotle chiles in adobo sauce pack lots of heat. If you're not a fan of spicy food, omit the chiles themselves and simply add 1 to 2 tablespoons of the adobo sauce for all the flavor of the chipotles without any of the heat.

Lentil Picadillo

PREP TIME: 5 minutes ✳ MANUAL: 20 minutes on high pressure ✳ RELEASE: Natural

TOTAL TIME: 50 minutes ✳ SERVES: 6 to 8

Lentil Picadillo is a tasty twist on classic picadillo, which is usually made with ground beef or ground pork. I use the same simple recipe that my *suegra* taught me how to make, except I've substituted dried lentils for the ground meat. This simple vegetarian picadillo is perfect if you're looking to add more meatless meals to your dinner rotation. Enjoy a bowl with a few warm corn tortillas on the side, or use it as a filling for tacos topped with onion, cilantro, and your favorite salsa.

4 Roma tomatoes, cut into quarters

2 to 3 serrano chiles, stemmed

2 garlic cloves, peeled

½ medium white onion, roughly chopped

1 pound dried lentils

4 medium carrots, peeled and diced

4 medium Yukon Gold potatoes, peeled and diced

6 cilantro sprigs (optional)

Coarse salt

1. In a blender, purée the tomatoes, chiles, garlic, onion, and 3 cups water until smooth.

2. Put the lentils in the Instant Pot®. Pour in the tomato purée. Add the carrots, potatoes, and cilantro (if using).

3. Lock the lid into place and set the steam release valve to sealed. Select Manual and set the timer for 20 minutes on high.

4. When cooking is complete, allow the pressure to release naturally. Unlock and remove the lid.

5. Season the picadillo with salt and serve immediately.

Option tip: Picadillo is an excellent way to sneak more veggies into your family's diet. Some of my favorites to add to picadillo are green beans, corn, squash, zucchini, and nopales.

Jackfruit al Pastor Tacos

PREP TIME: 10 minutes ✳ SAUTÉ: 3 minutes ✳ MANUAL: 10 minutes on high pressure
RELEASE: Natural ✳ TOTAL TIME: 45 minutes ✳ SERVES: 6 to 8

Jackfruit is all the rage right now on sites like Instagram and Pinterest, and with very good reason. This versatile fruit is a great vegetarian substitute for shredded meats in your favorite recipes. Inspired by a friend of mine, I decided to try my hand at making vegetarian *al pastor* tacos using jackfruit, and all I can say is that it was love at first bite.

1 tablespoon vegetable oil

1 medium white onion, thinly sliced

2 garlic cloves, minced

1 (7- to 8-pound) jackfruit, peeled, quartered, cored, and seeded, flesh scooped out by hand (see Ingredient tip below)

1 (30-ounce) can crushed pineapple with its juices

Juice of 1 orange

1 tablespoon white vinegar

1½ tablespoons ancho chile powder

½ tablespoon chipotle chile powder

1 teaspoon coarse salt

1 teaspoon crushed dried Mexican oregano

1 teaspoon ground cumin

½ teaspoon freshly ground black pepper

¼ teaspoon ground cloves

Corn tortillas

Chopped red onion, for garnish

Chopped fresh cilantro, for garnish

Salsa, for garnish

> CONTINUED

Jackfruit al Pastor Tacos

> CONTINUED

1. Set the Instant Pot® to Sauté and adjust to More for high. Heat the vegetable oil in the pot, add the onion and garlic, and sauté for 2 to 3 minutes, or until the onion is translucent.

2. Add the jackfruit, pineapple and its juices, and the orange juice.

3. Season the jackfruit mixture with the vinegar, chile powders, salt, oregano, cumin, pepper, and cloves.

4. Lock the lid into place and set the steam release valve to sealed. Select Manual and set the timer for 10 minutes on high.

5. When cooking is complete, allow the pressure to release naturally. Unlock and remove the lid.

6. Stir gently to combine. Heat the corn tortillas on a comal or griddle over medium heat until soft and pliable. Stack two tortillas per taco. Top with a couple of heaping tablespoons of the jackfruit *al pastor*. Garnish with chopped red onion, cilantro, and your favorite salsa.

Ingredient tip: Peeling a fresh jackfruit might seem intimidating, but freaketh not. It's actually a lot easier than you might think. The natural juices inside the jackfruit can sometimes be sticky, so I like to lightly coat my knife with cooking spray or coconut oil. Cut the jackfruit in quarters and pull out the center core. Scoop out the light yellowish-orange flesh using your hands, discarding any seeds or white fibrous (stringy) pieces. An important thing to remember is that jackfruit contains natural latex, so if you're allergic, take the proper precautions.

Chileatole Verde

SALSA VERDE SOUP

PREP TIME: 5 minutes ✳ SAUTÉ: 3 minutes ✳ MANUAL: 7 minutes on high pressure
RELEASE: Natural ✳ TOTAL TIME: 40 minutes ✳ SERVES: 4 to 6

Technically, *chileatole* is a savory *atole* (porridge) and should be served in mugs and sipped slowly to accompany tamales. Made with golden corn kernels simmered in a sumptuous salsa verde broth, *chileatole* can also be served as a light soup to enjoy with simple corn tortilla quesadillas for dipping. I like to top my Chileatole Verde with crumbled queso cotija, which plays perfectly with the salsa verde and corn.

1 tablespoon butter
1 tablespoon vegetable oil
½ medium white onion, finely chopped
1 garlic clove, minced
3 cups fresh corn kernels
2 cups Spicy Salsa Verde (page 24) or green enchilada sauce
2 cups chicken broth
Coarse salt
3 tablespoons masa harina
Crumbled queso cotija, for garnish

1. Set the Instant Pot® to Sauté and adjust to More for high. Heat the butter and vegetable oil in the pot until the butter is completely melted. Add the onion and garlic and sauté for 2 to 3 minutes, or until the onion is translucent.

2. Stir in the fresh corn kernels, salsa verde, chicken broth, and 1½ cups water. Season lightly with salt.

3. Lock the lid into place and set the steam release valve to sealed. Select Manual and set the timer for 7 minutes on high.

4. When cooking is complete, allow the pressure to release naturally. Unlock and remove the lid.

5. In a small bowl, dissolve the masa harina in ½ cup water. Immediately stir into the *chileatole* and stir for 1 to 2 minutes to thicken. Ladle into mugs. Sprinkle with crumbled queso cotija.

Substitution tip: Make *chileatole rojo* by substituting Salsa de Chile Colorado (page 21) or red enchilada sauce for the Spicy Salsa Verde.

Portobello Alambres

PORTOBELLO FAJITAS WITH BACON AND CHEESE

PREP TIME: 5 minutes ✳ SAUTÉ: 9 minutes ✳ MANUAL: 5 minutes on high pressure

RELEASE: Quick ✳ TOTAL TIME: 20 minutes ✳ SERVES: 6

Alambres are a traditional Mexican dish similar to fajitas, with the latter being more of a Tex-Mex dish. And if we're being completely honest, I prefer *alambres* to fajitas because *alambres* have bacon. Sizzling strips of bacon, onion, and an assortment of chiles can't be beat! *Alambres* can be made with beef, pork, chicken, shrimp, or even portobello mushrooms for a semi-meatless meal. For my vegetarian friends, you can omit the bacon, cheese, and sour cream.

6 bacon slices, cut into 1-inch pieces

1 medium white onion, thinly sliced

3 Roasted Poblano Peppers (page 134), peeled, seeded, and cut into thin strips

2 red bell peppers, thinly sliced

4 portobello mushrooms, stemmed and thinly sliced

1 teaspoon ground cumin

½ teaspoon freshly ground black pepper

Coarse salt

1½ cups shredded Manchego cheese

Warm flour tortillas, for serving (optional)

Guacamole (page 137), for garnish

Sour cream, for garnish

Salsa, for garnish

1. Set the Instant Pot® to Sauté and adjust to More for high. Fry the bacon in the pot for 4 to 6 minutes, or until golden and crisp. Add the onion, poblano peppers, and bell peppers. Sauté for 2 to 3 minutes, or until the onion is translucent. Add the portobello mushrooms; season with the cumin, pepper, and salt.

2. Lock the lid into place and set the steam release valve to sealed. Select Manual and set the timer for 5 minutes on high.

3. When cooking is complete, quick release the pressure. Unlock and remove the lid.

4. Sprinkle the Manchego cheese over the portobello mushrooms and peppers. Let set for 5 minutes, or until the cheese has melted completely. Serve the *alambres* with warm flour tortillas (if desired). Garnish with guacamole, sour cream, and your favorite salsa.

Option tip: Add a drained 20-ounce can of crushed pineapple in with the portobellos for a fun, tropical version I like to call *alambres Hawaianos*.

Ejotes en Salsa de Chile Colorado

GREEN BEANS IN RED CHILE SAUCE

PREP TIME: 5 minutes ✳ SAUTÉ: 4 minutes ✳ MANUAL: 5 minutes on high pressure
RELEASE: Natural ✳ TOTAL TIME: 24 minutes ✳ SERVES: 6

This is a dish my grandpa used to make to use up leftover red enchilada sauce. He loved to add *chile colorado* sauce to just about everything! He always prepared these saucy green beans as a side dish, but they were so good that I'd eat them on their own. My favorite way to enjoy them was for breakfast with a fried egg on top and cheesy refried beans on the side. Oh, so delicious!

1 tablespoon vegetable oil

¼ medium white onion, thinly sliced

2 tablespoons masa harina

1½ cups Salsa de Chile Colorado (page 21) or red enchilada sauce

12 ounces green beans, cut into 2-inch pieces

1. Set the Instant Pot® to Sauté and adjust to More for high. Heat the vegetable oil in the pot, add the onion, and sauté for 2 to 3 minutes, or until translucent. Sprinkle the masa harina over the onion and sauté for an additional 30 seconds. Whisk in 1 cup water and the chile sauce until the masa harina dissolves completely. Add the green beans.

2. Lock the lid into place and set the steam release valve to sealed. Select Manual and set the timer for 5 minutes on high.

3. When cooking is complete, allow the pressure to release naturally. Unlock and remove the lid.

4. Stir the beans gently to combine. Serve immediately.

Option tip: This recipe can also be made using cooked nopales.

Tamales de Rajas

ROASTED POBLANO PEPPER TAMALES

PREP TIME: 15 minutes, plus 30 minutes for soaking the corn husks
MANUAL: 25 minutes on high pressure ✳ RELEASE: Natural
TOTAL TIME: 1 hour 5 minutes ✳ MAKES: 12 tamales

If you've ever wanted to learn to make tamales at home, now is the time, because this is probably the easiest tamale recipe in the world. Using store-bought masa from your local Hispanic supermarket, you can enjoy home-cooked tamales any night of the week. These meatless ones are stuffed with roasted poblano pepper strips and queso fresco, and they are extremely popular in Mexico during Lent, when people refrain from eating meat on Fridays. In the state of Jalisco—the place I called home for 18 years—tamales are traditionally served topped with finely shredded lettuce and a mild tomato salsa.

16 large dried corn husks
3 pounds tamale masa
   (dough)
10 ounces queso fresco, cut
   into 12 slices
8 Roasted Poblano Peppers
   (page 134), peeled, seeded,
   and cut into thin strips
Caldillo de Jitomate
   (page 16) or Salsa
   Ranchera (page 23)
Shredded lettuce, for garnish

1. In a large plastic container, soak the dried corn husks in enough boiling water to cover them. Place a heavy lid or pan on top of the corn husks to keep them submerged. Let the corn husks soak for at least 30 minutes, or until soft and pliable. Rinse them with cold water to remove any dirt and residue, then pat dry with a kitchen towel.

2. In the Instant Pot®, pour 2 cups water and place the trivet inside.

3. Spoon about ¼ cup of masa onto each corn husk. Spread the masa until it's about ⅛ inch thick across two-thirds of the corn husk, leaving a ¼-inch space on one side and the top, and about a 3-inch space at the bottom.

4. Place a slice of queso fresco down the center of each masa-covered corn husk. Top each with a couple tablespoons of roasted poblano pepper strips.

5. Starting at the ¼-inch edge, gently fold each tamale in thirds, then tuck in the ends. Place the wrapped tamales seam-side down on a large plate.

6. Arrange the tamales vertically in the Instant Pot®, with the open ends facing upward.

7. Lock the lid into place and set the steam release valve to sealed. Select Manual and set the timer for 25 minutes on high.

8. When cooking is complete, allow the pressure to release naturally. Unlock and remove the lid.

9. While the tamales are steaming, in a small saucepan, warm the tomato sauce or salsa until heated through.

10. Let the tamales sit uncovered for 5 to 10 minutes before serving. To serve, remove the corn husks from the tamales. Top with shredded lettuce and ladle about ⅓ cup of the tomato sauce or salsa over each tamale. Enjoy!

Technique tip: Making tamales can seem overwhelming and complicated. I've tried to explain the steps in as much detail as possible. The process gets easier with each tamale you make. Practice really does make perfect.

Calabacitas

MEXICAN ZUCCHINI

PREP TIME: 5 minutes ✳ SAUTÉ: 3 minutes ✳ MANUAL: 5 minutes on high pressure
RELEASE: Quick ✳ TOTAL TIME: 15 minutes ✳ SERVES: 6

Calabacitas is a popular side dish in Mexico, but it is so good that I often eat it as a main dish either on its own or as a filling for tacos. This childhood favorite is super-simple, made with fresh Mexican *calabacitas* (a type of squash similar in flavor and texture to zucchini), onion, tomatoes, and corn. And it's even simpler when made in the Instant Pot®. Topped with crumbled queso fresco, Calabacitas makes for a light, delicious meatless meal you can enjoy for lunch or dinner.

1 tablespoon vegetable oil

½ medium white onion, finely chopped

1 serrano chile, seeded and finely chopped

5 medium *calabacitas* or zucchini, cut into 1-inch slices

3 Roma tomatoes, finely chopped

1 (15-ounce) can golden corn kernels, drained

Coarse salt

Freshly ground black pepper

1 cup crumbled queso cotija

1. Set the Instant Pot® to Sauté and adjust to More for high. Heat the vegetable oil in the pot, add the onion and chile, and sauté for 2 to 3 minutes, or until the onion is translucent. Stir in the *calabacitas*, tomatoes, and corn; season lightly with salt and pepper.

2. Lock the lid into place and set the steam release valve to sealed. Select Manual and set the timer for 5 minutes on high.

3. When cooking is complete, quick release the pressure. Unlock and remove the lid.

4. Sprinkle the crumbled queso cotija over the cooked *calabacitas*. Enjoy!

Substitution tip: Add even more color to this vibrant dish by substituting two yellow squash for the *calabacitas*.

". . . Calabacitas makes for a light, delicious meatless meal you can enjoy for lunch or dinner."

SALSA VERDE SHREDDED CHICKEN TAQUITOS, PAGE 92

CHAPTER 6

Chicken

Arroz con Pollo

CHICKEN WITH RICE

PREP TIME: 15 minutes ✳ **SAUTÉ:** 10 minutes ✳ **MANUAL:** 12 minutes on high pressure
RELEASE: Natural ✳ **TOTAL TIME:** 1 hour 5 minutes ✳ **SERVES:** 6

Arroz con Pollo is a classic Latin American dish, with each country—and each family, for that matter—having its own unique recipe. For mine, I like to use whole pieces of chicken (legs or thighs) that I season with chile powder, cumin, and oregano before adding the rice. This flavorful dish is filling all on its own, but it also goes well with *frijoles charros* (cowboy beans). Just don't forget the warm corn or flour tortillas.

1 tablespoon California
  chile powder
1 teaspoon ground cumin
1 teaspoon crushed dried
  Mexican oregano
1 teaspoon coarse salt, plus
  more for seasoning
½ teaspoon freshly ground
  black pepper
½ teaspoon onion powder
½ teaspoon garlic powder
6 boneless chicken thighs
3 tablespoons vegetable
  oil, divided

1 cup long-grain or
  jasmine rice
½ medium white onion,
  finely chopped
2 garlic cloves, minced
4 Roma tomatoes,
  finely chopped
1 cup chicken broth
1 (8-ounce) can
  tomato sauce
4 cilantro sprigs
Pico de Gallo Verde
  (page 135),
  for garnish (optional)
Pimiento-stuffed olives,
  sliced, for garnish (optional)

1. In a small bowl, combine the chile powder, cumin, oregano, salt, pepper, onion powder, and garlic powder. Sprinkle the spice mixture over the chicken thighs.

2. Set the Instant Pot® to Sauté and adjust to More for high. Heat 2 tablespoons of vegetable oil in the pot, add the chicken thighs, and fry for 5 to 7 minutes, or until golden brown. Transfer the chicken to a heat-proof plate.

3. In the Instant Pot®, heat the remaining 1 tablespoon of vegetable oil. Sauté the rice until light golden brown. Add the onion and garlic; sauté for 2 to 3 minutes, or just until the onion is translucent. Stir in the tomatoes.

4. Pour in the chicken broth and tomato sauce; season lightly with salt. Return the chicken to the Instant Pot®. Top with the cilantro.

5. Lock the lid into place and set the steam release valve to sealed. Select Manual and set the timer for 12 minutes on high.

6. When cooking is complete, allow the pressure to release naturally. Unlock and remove the lid.

7. Discard the cilantro. Serve immediately, garnished with *Pico de Gallo Verde* and pimiento-stuffed olive slices (if using).

Ingredient tip: For this recipe, I like to use skin-on chicken thighs, because my *abuelito* used to say that the skin is what adds the flavor.

Barbacoa de Pollo

CHICKEN BARBACOA

PREP TIME: 5 minutes ✳ MANUAL: 15 minutes on high pressure ✳ RELEASE: Natural
TOTAL TIME: 45 minutes ✳ SERVES: 6 to 8

Barbacoa is a Mexican delicacy made by slow-roasting meats in a spicy and tangy marinade. Barbacoa can be served on its own with refried beans and Mexican rice, or it can be chopped up and used as a filling for tacos. Traditionally, barbacoa is made with beef or pork, but it can also be made with lamb, goat, or chicken. For the adobo sauce, we're using the Salsa de Chile Colorado (page 21) as a base, then adding broth, herbs, and spices for extra flavor.

2½ pounds boneless, skinless chicken breast
3 garlic cloves, minced
1 cup Salsa de Chile Colorado (page 21) or red enchilada sauce
1 cup chicken broth
2 tablespoons white vinegar
1 teaspoon coarse salt
1 teaspoon crushed dried Mexican oregano
1 teaspoon ground cumin
½ teaspoon ground cinnamon
¼ teaspoon ground cloves
Pickled Red Onions (page 139), for garnish
Chopped fresh cilantro, for garnish

1. Put the chicken breast and garlic in the Instant Pot®. Pour in the chile sauce, broth, and vinegar. Season with the salt, oregano, cumin, cinnamon, and cloves.

2. Lock the lid into place and set the steam release valve to sealed. Select Manual and set the timer for 15 minutes on high.

3. When cooking is complete, allow the pressure to release naturally. Unlock and remove the lid.

4. Use two forks to shred the chicken breast in the pot. Serve immediately, garnished with pickled red onions and cilantro.

Substitution tip: Switch up the way you serve the chicken by using whole pieces, such as drumsticks, thighs, or leg quarters.

Caldo Tlalpeño

TLALPEÑO-STYLE CHICKEN AND CHICKPEA SOUP

PREP TIME: 10 minutes ✻ MANUAL: 15 minutes on high pressure ✻ RELEASE: Natural
TOTAL TIME: 45 minutes ✻ SERVES: 6 to 8

Caldo Tlalpeño is a traditional Mexican soup made with chicken and chickpeas in a light broth seasoned with onion, garlic, chipotle chiles, and epazote. Once served, the soup is garnished with cubes of avocado and queso fresco. The chipotles and epazote are what give the broth its distinct flavor. Epazote is a leafy herb with a pungent aroma and taste that is often used in soups and stews. If you are unable to find it, you can use cilantro instead.

½ medium white onion, quartered

2 garlic cloves, peeled

2 to 4 canned chipotle chiles in adobo sauce

2 cups chicken broth

2 pounds boneless, skinless chicken breasts, cut into 2-inch pieces

2 (15-ounce) cans chickpeas, drained

1 epazote leaf or 3 cilantro sprigs

1½ teaspoons coarse salt

Diced avocado, for garnish

Diced queso fresco, for garnish

Freshly squeezed lime juice, for garnish

Warm corn or flour tortillas, for serving (optional)

1. In a blender, purée the onion, garlic, 2 chipotle chiles, and the chicken broth until smooth. If desired, add the remaining 2 chipotles and process until smooth.

2. In the Instant Pot®, combine the chicken, chickpeas, and epazote. Pour in the onion purée and 4 cups water. Season with the salt.

3. Lock the lid into place and set the steam release valve to sealed. Select Manual and set the timer for 15 minutes on high.

4. When cooking is complete, allow the pressure to release naturally. Unlock and remove the lid.

5. Ladle the soup into bowls. Garnish with avocado, queso fresco, and a squeeze of fresh lime juice. Serve with warm tortillas (if desired).

Option tip: Some variations of this recipe include carrots and potatoes. To add more veggies to your soup, throw in 3 peeled and sliced medium carrots and 2 peeled and diced medium Yukon Gold potatoes with the chickpeas.

Carnitas de Pollo

CHICKEN CARNITAS

PREP TIME: 5 minutes ✳ **SAUTÉ:** 8 minutes ✳ **MANUAL:** 15 minutes on high pressure
RELEASE: Natural ✳ **TOTAL TIME:** 50 minutes ✳ **SERVES:** 6 to 8

Carnitas de Pollo is a delicious discovery I made upon returning to California after having lived for 18 years in Mexico. The chicken carnitas were flavorful, juicy, and tender, and I couldn't wait to re-create them at home. Cooking the carnitas in the Instant Pot® really locks in flavor and leaves the chicken super moist. Enjoy Carnitas de Pollo as a filling for tacos and other Mexican *antojitos* (street foods) or served alongside Frijoles Borrachos (page 32) and Classic Mexican Rice (page 28).

2 tablespoons *manteca* (pork lard) or vegetable oil

3 pounds boneless, skinless chicken breasts, cut into 2-inch pieces

1 cup freshly squeezed orange juice

¼ cup freshly squeezed lime juice

1½ teaspoons coarse salt

1 teaspoon crushed dried Mexican oregano

½ teaspoon freshly ground black pepper

1 medium white onion, thinly sliced

3 garlic cloves, minced

6 cilantro sprigs

Warm corn or flour tortillas, for serving (optional)

Lime wedges, for garnish

1. Set the Instant Pot to Sauté and adjust to More for high. Heat the *manteca* in the pot, add the chicken, and fry, stirring occasionally, for 6 to 8 minutes, or until golden brown.

2. Pour in the orange juice and lime juice. Season with the salt, oregano, and pepper. Top with the onion, garlic, and cilantro.

3. Lock the lid into place and set the steam release valve to sealed. Select Manual and set the timer for 15 minutes on high.

4. When cooking is complete, allow the pressure to release naturally. Unlock and remove the lid.

5. Using two forks, shred the chicken in the pot. Serve with warm tortillas (if desired) and garnish with lime wedges.

Technique tip: To crisp up the Carnitas de Pollo, transfer the shredded chicken from the Instant Pot® to a lightly greased baking dish. Bake in a 425°F oven for 5 to 7 minutes. Just before serving, drizzle the carnitas lightly with the broth they were cooked in.

Chipotle-Glazed Wings

PREP TIME: 10 minutes ✳ SAUTÉ: 15 minutes ✳ MANUAL: 10 minutes on high pressure
RELEASE: Quick ✳ TOTAL TIME: 35 minutes ✳ SERVES: 6 to 8

I am of the belief that everyone needs a good recipe for homemade chicken wings. They're the perfect appetizer for any party or casual gathering, because who doesn't love a good saucy and spicy wing? The two-ingredient glaze is one of my go-to sauces that I use for everything from stir-fries to glazed ham, but my favorite way to use it is on chicken wings. For this recipe, the wings cook in the Instant Pot® with a few seasonings, then finish in the oven for a few minutes with the sweet and spicy glaze.

3 pounds chicken wings

2 tablespoons vegetable oil

1 tablespoon chipotle chile powder

¾ teaspoon coarse salt

¼ teaspoon freshly ground black pepper

⅔ cup guava jam

4 to 6 tablespoons canned chipotle purée (see Ingredient tip)

1. Cut the chicken wings into three pieces, separating them at the joint; discard the wing tips.

2. Set the Instant Pot® to Sauté and adjust to More for high. Heat the vegetable oil in the pot. Working in batches, add the chicken wings and sauté, flipping once, for 6 to 8 minutes, or until light golden brown. As each batch of wings finishes cooking, transfer to a heat-proof plate. Season the wings with the chipotle powder, salt, and pepper.

3. Pour 1 cup of water into the Instant Pot®; place the trivet inside. Arrange the chicken wings on the trivet.

4. Lock the lid into place and set the steam release valve to sealed. Select Manual and set the timer for 10 minutes on high.

5. While the wings are cooking in the Instant Pot®, preheat the oven to 425°F. Lightly grease a baking sheet with cooking spray.

> CONTINUED

Chipotle-Glazed Wings

> CONTINUED

6. In a small bowl, mix the guava jam and canned chipotle purée.

7. When cooking is complete, quick release the pressure. Unlock and remove the lid.

8. Arrange the chicken wings in a single layer on the prepared baking sheet. Brush them with the guava-chipotle glaze. Bake the wings for 6 to 8 minutes, or until golden and crisp.

Ingredient tip: To make the canned chipotle purée, purée 1 (7-ounce) can chipotle chiles in adobo sauce in a blender until smooth. Store in an airtight container in the refrigerator for up to 2 weeks, or freeze in ice cube trays and then store in a plastic freezer bag for up to 3 months. Add 2 or 3 cubes of frozen chipotle purée to your favorite soups, pasta sauces, or Mexican dishes.

Mole de Guajolote

TURKEY MOLE

PREP TIME: 15 minutes ✳ SAUTÉ: 15 minutes ✳ MANUAL: 35 minutes on high pressure

RELEASE: Natural ✳ TOTAL TIME: 1 hour 30 minutes ✳ SERVES: 4

When I was little, Mole de Guajolote was reserved for special occasions—like weddings, christenings, first communions, and *quinceañeras*—and only when we visited Mexico. Traditional, completely from-scratch moles can be made with up to 40 different ingredients. But I didn't grow up with homemade mole. The one my grandparents used came from a glass jar, which they always saved to use as a drinking glass. Thanks to store-bought mole paste and the Instant Pot®, you can enjoy this fine-dining gem any night of the week.

3 tablespoons vegetable
  oil, divided
4 turkey legs
Coarse salt
Freshly ground black pepper
1 (8.25-ounce) jar mole paste
  (I use Doña María brand)
4 cups chicken broth
4 tablespoons sugar
Classic Mexican Rice (page 28),
  for serving
2 tablespoons toasted sesame
  seeds, for garnish

1. Set the Instant Pot® to Sauté and adjust to More for high. Heat 2 tablespoons of vegetable oil in the pot, then add the turkey legs, two at a time, and sauté, flipping a couple of times, for 6 to 8 minutes, or until light golden brown all over; season generously with salt and black pepper. As the turkey legs finish cooking, transfer to a heat-proof plate.

2. Heat the remaining 1 tablespoon of vegetable oil in the Instant Pot®. Add the mole paste and let it start to dissolve in the oil. Stir in the chicken broth, one cup at a time, until the mole paste has completely melted into the broth. Add the sugar and season with salt.

3. Return the turkey legs to the Instant Pot® and stir to coat them with the mole.

> CONTINUED

Mole de Guajolote

> CONTINUED

4. Lock the lid into place and set the steam release valve to sealed. Select Manual and set the timer for 35 minutes on high.

5. When cooking is complete, allow the pressure to release naturally. Unlock and remove the lid.

6. Serve the turkey mole with rice and garnish with the toasted sesame seeds

Option tip: Doctor up store-bought mole paste by stirring in one (or a combination) of the following: 1 (3-ounce) tablet Mexican chocolate, 2 tablespoons instant coffee granules, ¼ cup creamy peanut butter, and/or 1 (3-inch) cinnamon stick.

Pollo a la Cacerola

MEXICAN CHICKEN CACCIATORE

PREP TIME: 10 minutes ✴ SAUTÉ: 16 minutes ✴ MANUAL: 15 minutes on high pressure
RELEASE: Natural ✴ TOTAL TIME: 1 hour 5 minutes ✴ SERVES: 6

This is one of the dishes I make most in my *cocina* (kitchen). It's like a Mexican version of chicken cacciatore. Recipes for this comforting dish vary from family to family, but the base of the recipe is tender pieces of bone-in chicken simmered in a mild tomato salsa with onion, Hungarian wax peppers, and Mexican *calabacitas* (zucchini). Serve this comfort-food classic with Arroz Blanco (page 29) and warm tortillas.

4 tablespoons butter

6 chicken leg quarters

Coarse salt

Freshly ground black pepper

1 medium white onion,
   thinly sliced

2 Hungarian wax peppers

2 garlic cloves, minced

4 medium *calabacitas* or
   zucchini, cut into 1-inch slices

4 cilantro sprigs

1½ cups Caldillo de Jitomate
   (page 16) or tomato sauce

1 cup chicken broth

Arroz Blanco (page 29),
   for serving

Finely chopped fresh cilantro,
   for garnish

1. Set the Instant Pot® to Sauté and adjust to More for high. Heat the butter in the pot until completely melted. Add the chicken leg quarters, two or three at a time, and fry, flipping once, for 8 minutes, or until golden brown on both sides. Season generously with salt and pepper. As each batch of chicken pieces finishes cooking, transfer to a heat-proof plate.

2. Return all the chicken pieces to the Instant Pot®. Top with the onion, wax peppers, garlic, *calabacitas*, and cilantro sprigs. Pour in the tomato sauce and chicken broth.

3. Lock the lid into place and set the steam release valve to sealed. Select Manual and set the timer for 15 minutes on high.

4. When cooking is complete, allow the pressure to release naturally. Unlock and remove the lid.

5. Discard the cilantro sprigs. Serve immediately with rice. Garnish with chopped cilantro.

Option tip: Incorporate more veggies into your diet by adding 3 peeled and sliced medium carrots, 2 peeled and diced medium Yukon Gold potatoes, and 2 yellow squash cut into 1-inch slices in with the *calabacitas* and other vegetables in step 2.

Pollo a la Crema con Rajas

POBLANO CHICKEN

PREP TIME: 10 minutes ✻ SAUTÉ: 13 minutes ✻ MANUAL: 12 minutes on high pressure
RELEASE: Quick ✻ TOTAL TIME: 35 minutes ✻ SERVES: 6

Remember how I said that anytime you saw the words *rajas* and *crema* you'll know you're in for a treat? Well, it's even more true if you add chicken to the mix. Juicy pieces of chicken breast sautéed with roasted poblano strips, onion, garlic, sliced mushrooms, and golden corn kernels simmered in Mexican crema can be served on its own with Mexican rice, as a filling for tacos, quesadillas, or empanadas, or spooned over cooked pasta—which is my family's favorite way to enjoy Pollo a la Crema con Rajas (a.k.a. Poblano Chicken).

1 tablespoon extra-virgin
   olive oil
1 tablespoon butter
4 boneless, skinless chicken
   breasts, cut into thin strips
Coarse salt
Freshly ground black pepper
4 Roasted Poblano Peppers
   (page 134), peeled, seeded,
   and cut into thin strips
1 medium onion, thinly sliced
3 garlic cloves, minced
8 ounces button
   mushrooms, sliced
1 (15.5-ounce) can golden
   corn kernels, drained
1 cup Mexican crema or
   sour cream
⅓ cup whole milk
Crumbled *queso añejo* or
   cotija, for garnish

1. Set the Instant Pot® to Sauté and adjust to More for high. Heat the olive oil and butter in the pot until the butter has melted completely. Add the chicken and sauté for 6 to 8 minutes, or until it is no longer pink. Season generously with salt and pepper. Stir in the poblano peppers, onion, garlic, and mushrooms; sauté for 3 to 5 minutes, or until the onion is translucent.

2. Stir in the corn, Mexican crema, and milk.

3. Lock the lid into place and set the steam release valve to sealed. Select Manual and set the timer for 12 minutes on high.

4. When cooking is complete, quick release the pressure. Unlock and remove the lid.

5. Stir the chicken gently to combine. Garnish with crumbled *queso añejo*. Serve immediately.

Option tip: Poblano peppers aren't very spicy. To turn up the heat, add 1 seeded and chopped jalapeño pepper or 2 seeded and chopped serrano chiles in with the roasted poblano peppers and other vegetables in step 1.

Pollo Adobado con Papas

ADOBO CHICKEN AND POTATOES

PREP TIME: 5 minutes ✳ MANUAL: 35 minutes on high pressure ✳ RELEASE: Natural
TOTAL TIME: 1 hour 5 minutes ✳ SERVES: 6 to 8

This mouthwatering roast chicken and potato dish is one of those recipes that I never make the same way twice. For example, sometimes I purée the onion and garlic for the adobo sauce and other times I add the ingredients directly to the chicken and potato mixture. But that's the great thing about cooking, especially in the Instant Pot®: You can adapt recipes to fit your tastes and needs. Just make sure to have plenty of napkins on hand, because this chicken is finger-lickin' good.

3 pounds bone-in chicken breasts or thighs

6 medium Yukon Gold potatoes, cut into wedges

2 medium green bell peppers, seeded and roughly chopped

1 medium white onion, roughly chopped

3 garlic cloves, minced

1½ teaspoons coarse salt

1 teaspoon ground cumin

½ teaspoon freshly ground black pepper

1½ cups Salsa de Chile Colorado (page 21) or red enchilada sauce

1 cup freshly squeezed orange juice

Pickled jalapeño peppers, for garnish

Arroz Blanco (page 29), for serving

Ensalada de Nopales (Cactus Paddle Salad; see Option tip on page 115), for serving

1. In the Instant Pot®, combine the chicken, potatoes, bell peppers, onion, and garlic; season with the salt, cumin, and pepper.

2. Stir in the chile sauce and orange juice, making sure all the chicken and potato pieces are completely coated.

3. Lock the lid into place and set the steam release valve to sealed. Select Manual and set the timer for 35 minutes on high.

4. When cooking is complete, allow the pressure to release naturally. Unlock and remove the lid.

5. To serve, garnish with pickled jalapeños. Serve with rice and cactus salad.

Substitution tip: For a fun, tropical twist, stir in 1 (20-ounce) can crushed pineapple with the bell peppers and onion in step 1, and substitute pineapple juice for the orange juice in step 2.

Albóndigas de Pollo al Chipotle

CHIPOTLE CHICKEN MEATBALLS

PREP TIME: 10 minutes ✳ **MANUAL:** 15 minutes on high pressure ✳ **RELEASE:** Natural
TOTAL TIME: 45 minutes ✳ **SERVES:** 6 to 8

Albóndigas (meatballs) are my go-to comfort food because there are just so many ways to enjoy them, whether they're made from ground beef, pork, or chicken. One quick and easy way to make *albóndigas* is to simmer them in your favorite salsa, like this tomato-chipotle sauce. Just stir a couple tablespoons of the chipotle chile purée from the Chipotle-Glazed Wings (page 83) into the Caldillo de Jitomate (page 16), and dinner is set. Serve these meatballs with Arroz Blanco (page 29) or as the filling for a Mexican meatball sub (see Tip below).

2 pounds ground chicken
½ cup plain dried
   bread crumbs
⅓ cup long-grain or
   jasmine rice
⅓ cup old-fashioned oats
1 large egg
½ medium white onion,
   finely chopped
2 garlic cloves, minced
1 teaspoon coarse salt
½ teaspoon freshly ground
   black pepper
½ teaspoon crushed dried
   Mexican oregano
3 cups Caldillo de Jitomate
   (page 16) or tomato sauce
2 cups chicken broth
2 to 4 tablespoons canned
   chipotle purée (see
   Ingredient tip on page 84)
Arroz Blanco (page 29),
   for serving
Warm corn or flour tortillas,
   for serving (optional)

1. In a large bowl, mix the ground chicken, bread crumbs, rice, oats, egg, onion, garlic, salt, pepper, and oregano until well combined. Divide and shape the mixture into 2-inch meatballs; set aside.

2. In the Instant Pot®, combine the tomato sauce and chicken broth. Stir in 2 to 4 tablespoons of the chipotle purée, as desired. Carefully drop the meatballs into the sauce. Do not stir!

3. Lock the lid into place and set the steam release valve to sealed. Select Manual and set the timer for 15 minutes on high.

4. When cooking is complete, allow the pressure to release naturally. Unlock and remove the lid.

5. Stir gently to combine. Ladle into bowls over rice. Serve with warm tortillas (if desired).

Serving tip: To make Mexican meatball subs, split open a bolillo roll, without separating it completely, and toast lightly on a griddle until light golden brown. Spread the cut sides of the roll with Mexican crema. Spoon 3 to 4 meatballs down the center. Top with shredded Oaxaca and garnish with chopped fresh cilantro.

Shredded Chicken Tacos a la Mexicana

PREP TIME: 5 minutes ✳ **SAUTÉ:** 3 minutes ✳ **MANUAL:** 15 minutes on high pressure
RELEASE: Quick ✳ **TOTAL TIME:** 25 minutes ✳ **SERVES:** 6

Tacos de pollo a la Mexicana are some of the quickest and easiest tacos to make. A dish is called *"a la Mexicana"* because it is made with green chiles, white onion, and red tomatoes, which are representative of the colors of the Mexican flag. The chicken cooks up quickly in the Instant Pot®, resulting in tender, juicy pieces of meat that can easily be shredded with two forks. This filling is great for tacos, quesadillas, burritos, enchiladas, and tamales.

2 tablespoons vegetable oil

1 green bell pepper, chopped

1 to 2 serrano chiles, finely chopped

½ medium white onion, chopped

2 garlic cloves, minced

3 Roma tomatoes, chopped

1 cup chicken broth

2 pounds boneless, skinless chicken breast, cut into thin strips

Coarse salt

Freshly ground black pepper

¼ cup finely chopped fresh cilantro

24 corn tortillas, for serving

2 avocados, halved, pitted, peeled, and chopped, for garnish

Mexican crema, for garnish

Freshly squeezed lime juice, for garnish

1. Set the Instant Pot® to Sauté and adjust to More for high. Heat the vegetable oil in the pot, add the bell pepper, chiles, onion, and garlic, and sauté for 2 to 3 minutes, or until the onion is translucent.

2. Stir in the tomatoes and chicken broth. Arrange the chicken breast strips on top of the vegetable mixture. Season with salt and pepper.

3. Lock the lid into place and set the steam release valve to sealed. Select Manual and set the timer for 15 minutes on high.

4. When cooking is complete, quick release the pressure. Unlock and remove the lid.

5. Using two forks, shred the chicken. Stir in the cilantro.

6. Heat the corn tortillas on a comal or griddle until soft and pliable. Stack two corn tortillas per taco. Spoon 2 to 3 heaping tablespoons of the shredded chicken filling down the center of each taco. Garnish with chopped avocado, Mexican crema, and a squeeze of fresh lime juice.

Freezer tip: Have leftovers? This filling can be frozen in an airtight container or freezer bag for up to 3 months. Let defrost overnight in the refrigerator before using.

Salsa Verde Shredded Chicken Taquitos

PREP TIME: 5 minutes   *   MANUAL: 15 minutes on high pressure   *   RELEASE: Natural

TOTAL TIME: 45 minutes   *   SERVES: 6 to 8

This has to be one of the easiest recipes in the entire book. It was one of my favorite childhood dishes, and one of the only things I ever ordered when we went out to eat. These taquitos feature flavorful shredded chicken simmered in salsa verde, then wrapped in a corn tortilla that is fried until golden and crisp. The quick and easy filling can be used for tacos, burritos, enchiladas, and/or tamales.

2¼ pounds boneless, skinless chicken breasts

½ medium white onion, finely chopped

2 garlic cloves, minced

4 cilantro sprigs

1½ cups Spicy Salsa Verde (page 24) or green enchilada sauce

1 cup chicken broth

1 teaspoon coarse salt

12 to 16 corn tortillas

1 cup vegetable oil

Shredded lettuce, for garnish

Guacamole (page 137), for garnish

Crumbled queso cotija, for garnish

1. In the Instant Pot®, combine the chicken, onion, garlic, and cilantro. Pour the salsa verde and chicken broth on top; season with the salt.

2. Lock the lid into place and set the steam release valve to sealed. Select Manual and set the timer for 15 minutes on high.

3. When cooking is complete, allow the pressure to release naturally. Unlock and remove the lid.

4. Discard the cilantro sprigs. Using two forks, shred the chicken in the pot.

5. Heat the corn tortillas on a comal or griddle over medium-high heat until soft and pliable. Spoon 2 to 3 heaping tablespoons of the shredded chicken mixture down the center of each tortilla. Roll the taquitos up tightly, securing with a toothpick if necessary.

6. Heat the vegetable oil in a medium skillet over high heat. Fry the taquitos, 3 to 4 at a time, until golden and crisp. As you finish frying each batch, transfer the taquitos to a paper towel–lined plate to drain any excess oil.

7. To serve, arrange 2 or 3 taquitos per plate. Garnish with shredded lettuce, guacamole, and queso cotija.

Substitution tip: Have fun playing with different flavors for this easy shredded chicken filling by switching out the salsa verde for Salsa Ranchera (page 23) or Salsa Gemma (page 22).

Sopa de Lima

MEXICAN LIME SOUP

PREP TIME: 10 minutes ✻ SAUTÉ: 3 minutes ✻ MANUAL: 15 minutes on high pressure
RELEASE: Natural ✻ TOTAL TIME: 50 minutes ✻ SERVES: 6 to 8

Sopa de Lima is a spicy and tangy chicken soup that originated in the state of
Yucatán. If you're tired of making the same old chicken soup, liven up your dinner
rotation with this souped-up version flavored with cinnamon, lime juice, and
Hungarian wax peppers. While this is a traditional Mexican soup, my recipe is
a mash-up of the different variations I grew up eating. For instance, I sauté onion,
Hungarian wax peppers, garlic, and tomatoes to add more flavor to the broth, just
like my *suegra* did.

2 tablespoons vegetable oil

1 medium white onion,
  finely chopped

3 Hungarian wax peppers,
  seeded and thinly sliced

3 garlic cloves, minced

3 Roma tomatoes, chopped

2 pounds boneless, skinless
  chicken breasts, cut into
  2-inch pieces

4 cilantro sprigs

2 cups chicken broth

Juice of 4 limes

1 (3-inch) cinnamon stick

1½ teaspoons coarse salt

½ teaspoon freshly ground
  black pepper

Cubed avocado, for garnish

Chopped queso fresco,
  for garnish

Mexican crema, for garnish

Fried tortilla strips,
  for garnish

Freshly squeezed lime juice,
  for garnish

Warm corn or flour tortillas,
  for serving (optional)

1. Set the Instant Pot® to Sauté and adjust to More for high. Heat the vegetable oil in the pot, add the onion, wax peppers, and garlic, and sauté for 2 to 3 minutes, or until the onion is just translucent. Stir in the tomatoes and sauté for an additional 30 seconds.

2. Add the chicken breasts and cilantro. Pour in 4 cups of water, the chicken broth, and lime juice. Add the cinnamon stick and season with the salt and pepper.

3. Lock the lid into place and set the steam release valve to sealed. Select Manual and set the timer for 15 minutes on high.

4. When cooking is complete, allow the pressure to release naturally. Unlock and remove the lid.

5. Ladle the soup into bowls. Garnish with avocado, queso fresco, a drizzling of Mexican crema, fried tortilla strips, and a squeeze of fresh lime juice. Serve with warm tortillas (if desired).

Substitution tip: For an even spicier, more authentic broth, substitute 1 seeded and thinly sliced habanero chile for the Hungarian wax peppers.

Sopa de Tortilla

TORTILLA SOUP

PREP TIME: 10 minutes ✳ **MANUAL:** 15 minutes on high pressure ✳ **RELEASE:** Natural
TOTAL TIME: 30 minutes ✳ **SERVES:** 6 to 8

Tortilla soup (also known as *sopa Azteca*) is one of my favorite chicken soups. Not only is it tasty and delicious, it's also super easy to make. It's because of soups like this that I always make large batches of my favorite salsas from chapter 2 to use in various recipes. The chicken is simmered in a dried chile and tomato broth, and the soup is served loaded with garnishes for added flavor. This is another soup I prefer to serve with a crusty bolillo roll to dip into the broth.

½ medium white
   onion, peeled
2 garlic cloves, peeled
2 cups chicken broth
2 pounds boneless, skinless
   chicken breasts, cut into
   2-inch pieces
4 cilantro sprigs
1 cup Salsa de Chile
   Colorado (page 21) or
   red enchilada sauce
1 cup Caldillo de Jitomate
   (page 16) or tomato sauce
1½ teaspoons coarse salt
Chopped avocado,
   for garnish
Chopped queso fresco,
   for garnish
Mexican crema, for garnish
Fried tortilla strips,
   for garnish
Freshly squeezed lime juice,
   for garnish
Warm corn or flour tortillas,
   for serving (optional)

1. In a blender, purée the onion, garlic, and chicken broth until smooth.

2. In the Instant Pot®, arrange the chicken breast pieces and cilantro sprigs. Pour in the onion purée, chile sauce, tomato sauce, and 3 cups of water. Season with the salt.

3. Lock the lid into place and set the steam release valve to sealed. Select Manual and set the timer for 15 minutes on high.

4. When cooking is complete, allow the pressure to release naturally. Unlock and remove the lid.

5. Ladle the soup into bowls. Garnish with avocado, queso fresco, a drizzling of Mexican crema, fried tortilla strips, and a squeeze of fresh lime juice. Serve with warm tortillas (if desired).

Substitution tip: Transform this tortilla soup recipe into salsa verde tortilla soup by substituting 2 cups Spicy Salsa Verde (page 24) or green enchilada sauce for the red enchilada and tomato sauces.

"The chicken is simmered in a dried chile and tomato broth, and the soup is served loaded with garnishes for added flavor."

PORK CARNITAS, PAGE 105

CHAPTER 7

Beef & Pork

99

Asado de Boda

MEXICAN WEDDING PORK ROAST

PREP TIME: 10 minutes ✳ SAUTÉ: 10 minutes ✳ MANUAL: 30 minutes on high pressure
RELEASE: Natural ✳ TOTAL TIME: 1 hour 15 minutes ✳ SERVES: 6 to 8

Asado de Boda is a traditional roast pork dish popular in the Mexican state of Zacatecas. It was often reserved for special occasions, especially weddings, hence the name, which means "wedding roast." Asado de Boda is roasted pork loin simmered in a luxurious ancho chile sauce seasoned with Mexican chocolate, sugar, orange zest, black pepper, cinnamon, cloves, and bay leaves. Because your Instant Pot® does all the work in just a fraction of the time it usually takes, you can enjoy this sumptuous dish any night of the week.

2 tablespoons lard or vegetable oil

2¼ pounds pork loin, cut into 2-inch pieces

1 (3-ounce) Mexican chocolate tablet, cut into 8 wedges

2 cups Salsa de Chile Colorado (page 21) or red enchilada sauce

4 tablespoons sugar

1 tablespoon finely grated orange zest

1 teaspoon coarse salt

½ teaspoon freshly ground black pepper

1 teaspoon ground cinnamon

¼ teaspoon ground cloves

2 bay leaves

3 tablespoons masa harina

Classic Mexican Rice (page 28), for serving

Frijoles Meneados (page 33), for serving

Warm corn tortillas, for serving

1. Set the Instant Pot® to sauté and adjust to More for high. Heat the lard in the pot, add the pork loin, and sauté, stirring occasionally, for 6 to 8 minutes, or until light golden brown. Transfer the pork to a heat-proof plate.

2. In the Instant Pot®, heat the chocolate for 1 to 2 minutes, or until it just starts to soften. Stir in 1 cup of water. Continue to cook, stirring constantly, until the chocolate has melted completely. Stir in the chile sauce, sugar, orange zest, salt, pepper, cinnamon, and cloves. Return the pork loin to the pot. Top with the bay leaves.

3. Lock the lid into place and set the steam release valve to sealed. Select Manual and set the timer for 30 minutes on high.

4. When cooking is complete, allow the pressure to release naturally. Unlock and remove the lid. Remove and discard the bay leaves.

5. In a small bowl, dissolve the masa harina in ¼ cup water. Immediately stir into the pork mixture in the Instant Pot®. Serve with rice, beans, and warm corn tortillas.

Substitution tip: Traditionally, Asado de Boda is made by frying the pork loin in *manteca* (lard), which adds more of that delicious fried pork flavor, but you can also use vegetable oil.

Beer-Braised Beef Roast

PREP TIME: 10 minutes ✳ SAUTÉ: 8 minutes ✳ MANUAL: 60 minutes on high pressure
RELEASE: Natural ✳ TOTAL TIME: 1 hour 30 minutes ✳ SERVES: 6 to 8

This is one of my go-to recipes when I want juicy, succulent shredded beef to use as a filling for tacos, burritos, and even tamales. Cumin, Mexican beer, Maggi Jugo (a Mexican seasoning sauce), and Worcestershire sauce come together in a flavorful brisket that's so tasty, you'll be licking your fingers clean. No matter how you decide to serve up your brisket, don't forget the Classic Mexican Rice (page 28), the Frijoles Meneados (page 33), and the warm tortillas (when it comes to this shredded beef, flour tortillas are best!).

3 tablespoons ancho
   chile powder
1½ teaspoons crushed dried
   Mexican oregano
1 teaspoon ground cumin
¾ teaspoon coarse salt
¾ teaspoon freshly ground
   black pepper
3 pounds beef chuck roast,
   cut into 3-inch pieces
2 tablespoons vegetable oil
1 large white onion,
   thinly sliced
3 garlic cloves, minced
5 cilantro sprigs
1 (12-ounce) bottle
   Mexican beer

¼ cup freshly squeezed
   lime juice
1 tablespoon Maggi Jugo
   seasoning sauce (see
   Ingredient tip)
1 tablespoon
   Worcestershire sauce
Chopped fresh cilantro,
   for garnish
Arroz Verde (page 30) or
   Classic Mexican Rice
   (page 28), for serving
Frijoles Meneados (page 33),
   for serving
Chopped red onion,
   for garnish
Flour tortillas, for serving
   (optional)

1. In a small bowl, combine the chile powder, oregano, cumin, salt, and pepper. Sprinkle the spice rub over the chuck roast.

2. Set the Instant Pot® to Sauté and adjust to More for high. Heat the vegetable oil in the pot, add the meat, and fry for 6 to 8 minutes, or until lightly golden brown all over. Add the sliced onion, garlic, and cilantro sprigs. Pour in the beer, lime juice, Maggi Jugo seasoning sauce, and Worcestershire sauce.

3. Lock the lid into place and set the steam release valve to sealed. Select Manual and set the timer for 60 minutes on high.

4. When cooking is complete, allow the pressure to release naturally. Unlock and remove the lid.

5. Using two forks, shred the meat in the pot. Serve with rice and beans, or, if desired, use the beef as a filling for tacos. Garnish with chopped red onion and cilantro.

Ingredient tip: Maggi Jugo is a flavorful, umami-rich sauce used in roasted and grilled meat dishes, as well as in cocktails. You can find it in the Latin foods aisle of your grocery store, or in the same aisle as you would find soy sauce.

Beef Shank Barbacoa

PREP TIME: 5 minutes ✳ MANUAL: 45 minutes on high pressure ✳ RELEASE: Natural

TOTAL TIME: 1 hour 15 minutes ✳ SERVES: 6

Barbacoa de res is a traditional Mexican dish with tender pieces of beef served in a dried-chile broth seasoned with ground cumin and crushed oregano. You won't believe how easy this barbacoa is to make, and you can serve it a number of ways, so you'll never get bored with it. You can serve it the traditional way, with lots of chile broth topped with chopped onion and cilantro. Or you can serve the beef shanks whole, osso buco–style, with mashed potatoes and a chile broth gravy. (Yum!) Then, if you have any leftovers, finely chop the meat and spoon onto warm corn tortillas for tacos de barbacoa.

3 pounds beef shanks or boneless country-style beef ribs

¾ teaspoon coarse salt

½ teaspoon ground cumin

½ teaspoon freshly ground black pepper

¼ teaspoon crushed dried oregano

2 garlic cloves, thinly sliced

½ medium white onion, thinly sliced

1½ cups Salsa de Chile Colorado (page 21) or red enchilada sauce

1 (10.5-ounce) can beef broth

Chopped onion, for garnish

Chopped fresh cilantro, for garnish

Warm corn tortillas, for serving (optional)

1. In the Instant Pot, combine the beef shanks, salt, cumin, pepper, and oregano. Top with the garlic and onion. Pour in the chile sauce, beef broth, and 1 cup water.

2. Lock the lid into place and set the steam release valve to sealed. Select Manual and set the timer for 45 minutes on high.

3. When cooking is complete, allow the pressure to release naturally. Unlock and remove the lid.

4. To serve, break up the beef shanks (or serve them whole) and ladle the chile broth over the meat. Garnish with chopped onion and cilantro. Serve with warm corn tortillas (if desired).

Option tip: For tacos, finely chop the beef shanks and serve on warm tortillas. Spoon the chile broth over the meat in place of salsa, and garnish the tacos with chopped onion and cilantro. Enjoy!

Pork Carnitas

PREP TIME: 10 minutes ✳ SAUTÉ: 10 minutes ✳ MANUAL: 25 minutes on high pressure

RELEASE: Natural ✳ TOTAL TIME: 1 hour 10 minutes ✳ YIELD: 6 to 8 servings

Traditionally, carnitas are slow cooked for hours in a large copper *cazo* (pot) filled with *manteca de cerdo* (pork lard) and stirred occasionally with an oversize (4- to 6-foot) wooden spoon. While the resulting little pieces of crispy fried pork are absolutely irresistible, the reality is: Ain't no one got time for that. But with the Instant Pot® you can enjoy a healthier and more flavorful version of carnitas in about an hour. Make a feast out of this easy weeknight meal by serving with Frijoles Borrachos (page 32) and Classic Mexican Rice (page 28), or serve the carnitas as a simple taco filling and top with chopped onion, cilantro, a squeeze of fresh lime juice, and your favorite salsa.

2 tablespoons *manteca* (pork lard) or vegetable oil

2¼ pounds pork shoulder roast or Boston butt, cut into 2-inch pieces

1 teaspoon coarse salt

1 teaspoon ground cumin

½ teaspoon freshly ground black pepper

1 cup freshly squeezed orange juice

¼ cup freshly squeezed lime juice

2 bay leaves

1. Set the Instant Pot® to sauté and adjust to More for high. Heat the *manteca* in the pot until completely melted. Add the pork and fry for 6 to 8 minutes, or until light golden brown. Season with the salt, cumin, and pepper. Add the orange and lime juices and top with the bay leaves.

2. Lock the lid into place and set the steam release valve to sealed. Select Manual and set the timer for 25 minutes on high.

3. When cooking is complete, allow the pressure to release naturally. Unlock and remove the lid. Remove and discard the bay leaves.

4. Using two forks, shred the pork carnitas in the pot. Enjoy!

Option tip: To crisp up your carnitas, spread them out on an ungreased baking sheet. Bake in a 425°F oven for 8 to 10 minutes, or until golden and crisp.

Pork Chile Colorado

PREP TIME: 10 minutes   ✳   SAUTÉ: 12 minutes   ✳   MANUAL: 25 minutes on high pressure
RELEASE: Natural   ✳   TOTAL TIME: 1 hour 15 minutes   ✳   SERVES: 6 to 8

This was my grandpa's signature dish. It reminded him of his childhood in the rural mountains of Chihuahua, where the classic Mexican dish is one of the state's most treasured recipes. I've made only one change to my grandfather's original recipe: making my own Salsa de Chile Colorado (page 21) with dried ancho chiles instead of using the canned enchilada sauce Pappy always used. I've stayed true to his recipe by adding plenty of his favorite ingredients, like the oregano and cumin in the chile sauce, as well as garlic, nopales, and pinto beans. This dish can be served as a stew or as a filling for tacos and/or burritos.

2 tablespoons *manteca* (pork lard) or vegetable oil
2¼ pounds pork loin, cut in 1-inch chunks
½ medium onion, thinly sliced
3 garlic cloves, minced
¾ teaspoon coarse salt
½ teaspoon freshly ground black pepper
1½ cups roughly chopped cooked nopales
1½ cups cooked pinto beans
¼ cup masa harina
2 cups Salsa de Chile Colorado (page 21) or red enchilada sauce
Warm corn tortillas, for serving (optional)

1. Set the Instant Pot® to Sauté and adjust to More for high. Heat the *manteca* in the pot until completely melted. Add the pork loin and fry for 6 to 8 minutes, or until lightly golden brown. Stir in the onion and garlic; sauté for 2 to 3 minutes, or just until the onion is translucent. Season with the salt and pepper. Add the cooked nopales and pinto beans.

2. In a small bowl, mix the masa harina with 1 cup water. Pour into the Instant Pot® and add the chile sauce.

3. Lock the lid into place and set the steam release valve to sealed. Select Manual and set the timer for 25 minutes on high.

4. When cooking is complete, allow the pressure to release naturally. Unlock and remove the lid.

5. Serve the pork immediately with warm corn tortillas (if desired).

Substitution tip: Use beef chuck roast instead of the pork loin to make the filling for Gramm's Famous Shredded Beef Chile Colorado Tamales (page 111). Increase the cook time to 45 minutes on high.

Pork Chile Verde

PREP TIME: 10 minutes ✳ **SAUTÉ:** 12 minutes ✳ **MANUAL:** 25 minutes on high pressure
RELEASE: Natural ✳ **TOTAL TIME:** 1 hour 10 minutes ✳ **SERVES:** 6 to 8

Just like Pork Chile Colorado (page 106), this comforting classic made with juicy pieces of pork meat simmered in a tangy salsa verde with corn and *calabacitas* has been a favorite since childhood. Pappy often made his pork chile verde with potatoes and nopales, but I like the pop of color from the golden corn on the cob and dark green of the Mexican *calabacitas*. This dish can be served as a stew with warm corn tortillas and a side of creamy refried beans, but it also makes a delicious filling for tamales.

2 tablespoons *manteca* (pork lard) or vegetable oil

2½ pounds pork loin, cut into 2-inch pieces

¾ teaspoon coarse salt

¼ teaspoon freshly ground black pepper

½ medium white onion, thinly sliced

3 garlic cloves, minced

2 ears corn, husks removed, cut into 2-inch pieces

6 medium Mexican *calabacitas*, cut into 1-inch slices

2 cups Spicy Salsa Verde (page 24) or green enchilada sauce

Warm corn tortillas, for serving (optional)

Frijoles Meneados (page 33), for serving (optional)

1. Set the Instant Pot® to Sauté and adjust to More for high. Heat the *manteca* in the pot until completely melted. Add the pork and fry for 6 to 8 minutes, or until light golden brown. Season with the salt and pepper. Add the onion and garlic; sauté for an additional 2 to 3 minutes, or just until the onion is translucent. Add the corn, *calabacitas*, salsa verde, and ½ cup water. Stir gently to combine.

2. Lock the lid into place and set the steam release valve to sealed. Select Manual and set the timer for 25 minutes on high.

3. When cooking is complete, allow the pressure to release naturally. Unlock and remove the lid.

4. Serve the pork immediately with warm corn tortillas and refried beans (if desired).

Option tip: If making Pork Chile Verde as a filling for tamales, increase the amount of meat to 3 pounds and omit the corn and *calabacitas*. After removing the lid of the Instant Pot®, use two forks to shred the pork.

Pork Tinga Tostadas

PREP TIME: 10 minutes * SAUTÉ: 10 minutes * MANUAL: 25 minutes on high pressure
RELEASE: Natural * TOTAL TIME: 1 hour 10 minutes * SERVES: 6 to 8

These tostadas are a quick and easy dinner option, perfect for any night of the week! Add a few crunchy tostada shells, shredded lettuce, Mexican crema, and crumbled cotija cheese, and you've got a meal that tastes like you spent hours in the kitchen. Traditionally, *tinga* is made with braised chicken in a tomato-chipotle sauce, but for this tasty pork version, I like to add just a hint of tanginess by using a tomatillo-based salsa.

1 (28-ounce) can mild green enchilada sauce

2 or 3 canned chipotles chiles in adobo sauce

1 tablespoon vegetable oil

8 ounces Mexican pork chorizo

1 medium white onion, thinly sliced

2 garlic cloves, minced

2¼ pounds pork loin, cut into 2-inch pieces

¾ teaspoon coarse salt

¼ teaspoon freshly ground black pepper

Tostada shells, for serving

Shredded lettuce, for garnish

Mexican crema, for garnish

Crumbled queso cotija, for garnish

1. In a blender, purée the enchilada sauce and chipotle chiles until smooth.

2. Set the Instant Pot® to Sauté and adjust to More for high. Heat the vegetable oil in the pot, add the chorizo, and fry for 5 to 7 minutes, breaking up the meat with the back of a wooden spoon, until cooked through. Stir in the onion and garlic; sauté for 2 to 3 minutes, or until the onion is translucent.

3. Pour in the chipotle purée. Add the pork loin. Season with the salt and black pepper.

4. Lock the lid into place and set the steam release valve to sealed. Select Manual and set the timer for 25 minutes on high.

5. When cooking is complete, allow the pressure to release naturally. Unlock and remove the lid.

6. Using two forks, shred the pork meat. Spoon 3 or 4 heaping tablespoonfuls of pork *tinga* atop tostada shells. Garnish with shredded lettuce, Mexican crema, and crumbled queso cotija.

Option tip: *Tinga* also makes for a tantalizing torta filling. Spread a lightly toasted bolillo roll with Mexican crema. Spoon 3 or 4 heaping tablespoonfuls of *tinga* inside each roll. Garnish with shredded lettuce, sliced red onion, fresh cilantro, and crumbled queso cotija.

Ropa Vieja a la Mexicana

MEXICAN-STYLE ROPA VIEJA

PREP TIME: 10 minutes ✳ **SAUTÉ:** 10 minutes ✳ **MANUAL:** 30 minutes on high pressure
RELEASE: Natural ✳ **TOTAL TIME:** 1 hour 15 minutes ✳ **YIELD:** 6 to 8 servings

Ropa Vieja is a classic Cuban dish made with shredded beef in a flavorful tomato-based sauce with roasted red peppers and olives that gets its name because it looks like a pile of old clothes. One of my childhood best friends (Max) was Cuban, and his mom made Ropa Vieja often to share when my grandparents and I would visit. Pappy (my grandpa) loved it and immediately tried to re-create it at home, giving it a slight Mexican twist by adding his favorite Anaheim chiles in place of the red peppers. Ropa Vieja is still one of my favorites, to which I've added a few extra ingredients—like paprika, Hungarian wax peppers, tomatoes, and black olives—to enhance the already rich flavor of this classic dish.

2½ pounds flank steak

1 teaspoon coarse salt

1 teaspoon paprika

½ teaspoon freshly ground black pepper

2 tablespoons vegetable oil

2 Roasted Poblano Peppers (page 134), peeled, seeded, and cut into thin strips

2 Hungarian wax peppers, seeded and thinly sliced

2 Anaheim chiles, seeded and thinly sliced

1 medium white onion, thinly sliced

2 garlic cloves, minced

3 Roma tomatoes, seeded and thinly sliced

1 (8-ounce) can pitted black olives, drained

1 (10.5-ounce) can beef broth

1½ cups Caldillo de Jitomate (page 16) or tomato sauce

2 dried bay leaves

Arroz Blanco (page 29), for serving

Warm corn or flour tortillas, for serving (optional)

> CONTINUED

Ropa Vieja a la Mexicana

> CONTINUED

1. Season the flank steak with the salt, paprika, and pepper. Set the Instant Pot® to Sauté and adjust to More for high. Heat the vegetable oil in the pot, add the flank steak, and sauté, flipping once, for 5 to 7 minutes, or until golden brown. Transfer the steak to a heat-proof plate.

2. Add the poblano peppers, wax peppers, chiles, onion, and garlic to the pot. Sauté for 2 to 3 minutes, or just until the onion is translucent. Add the tomatoes, black olives, beef broth, and tomato sauce. Return the steak to the pot. Top with the bay leaves.

3. Lock the lid into place and set the steam release valve to sealed. Select Manual and set the timer for 30 minutes on high.

4. When cooking is complete, allow the pressure to release naturally. Unlock and remove the lid. Remove and discard the bay leaves.

5. Using two forks, shred the steak in the pot. Serve with rice and warm tortillas (if desired).

Option tip: This recipe makes a tasty filling for tamales, quesadillas, tacos, empanadas, and enchiladas.

Gramm's Famous Shredded Beef Chile Colorado Tamales

PREP TIME: 20 minutes, plus 30 minutes for soaking the corn husks
MANUAL: 30 minutes on high pressure ✶ RELEASE: Natural
TOTAL TIME: 1 hour 15 minutes ✶ MAKES: 24 tamales

If you were to ask me my favorite thing to make in the Instant Pot®, hands down it has to be tamales! Making them at home, completely from scratch, is a labor of love. First you have to prepare the filling, soak the corn husks, prepare the masa (dough), spread the masa onto the corn husks, add the filling, wrap up your tamales, and, finally—the hardest part—wait for them to cook. Thankfully, with the Instant Pot® it takes only an hour for the tamales to be completely cooked through.

When it comes to my favorite kind of tamales, well, of course it's the ones I grew up with: my *abuelita*'s famous tamales filled with tender, juicy pieces of shredded beef (or pork) in a rich Salsa de Chile Colorado (page 21), tucked inside a soft, billowy corn masa. Hidden inside each one was Gramm's secret ingredient: black olives! Adding 2 or 3 olives to each tamale results in a unique flavor, and it's no wonder these are still my favorite tamales.

24 dried corn husks
4 cups masa harina (I use regular Maseca brand)
1½ teaspoons baking powder
1 teaspoon coarse salt
1 cup *manteca* (pork lard) or shortening
3 cups very warm beef broth

4½ cups shredded beef chile colorado (see Substitution tip, page 106)
2 to 3 (6-ounce) cans pitted black olives, drained
2 cups Caldillo de Jitomate (page 16) or Salsa Ranchera (page 23)
Shredded lettuce, for serving

> CONTINUED

Gramm's Famous Shredded Beef Chile Colorado Tamales

> CONTINUED

1. In a large plastic container, soak the dried corn husks in enough boiling water to cover them. Place a heavy lid or pan on top of the corn husks to keep them submerged. Let them soak for at least 30 minutes, or until soft and pliable. Rinse the corn husks with cold water to remove any dirt and residue, then pat them dry with a kitchen towel.

2. In a medium bowl, combine the masa harina, baking powder, and salt; set aside. In a large mixing bowl, cream the *manteca* with an electric mixer on medium-high speed until light and fluffy. (Light and fluffy *manteca* makes for light and fluffy tamales.)

3. With the mixer still on medium-high, slowly add in the masa harina mixture, one cup at a time, until no dry bits are visible. The mixture will be grainy. Reduce the mixer speed to low and stir in the warm beef broth until it has all been absorbed. Using your hands, press the mixture together to form a dough.

4. Add 2 cups of water to the Instant Pot®; place the trivet inside.

5. Spoon about ¼ cup of dough onto each corn husk, spreading it about ⅛ inch thick across two-thirds of the corn husk. Leave a ¼-inch space on one side and at the top, and about a 3-inch space at the bottom.

6. Place 2 to 3 tablespoons of the shredded beef filling down the center of the masa-covered cornhusk. Top with 2 or 3 black olives.

7. Starting at the ¼-inch edge, gently fold each tamale in thirds, then tuck in the ends. Place the wrapped tamales seam-side down on a large plate.

8. Arrange the tamales vertically in the Instant Pot®, with the open ends facing upward.

9. Lock the lid into place and set the steam release valve to sealed. Select manual and set the timer for 30 minutes on high.

10. While the tamales are steaming, warm the tomato sauce or salsa in a small saucepan until heated through.

11. When cooking on the tamales is complete, allow the pressure to release naturally. Unlock and remove the lid. Let the tamales sit, uncovered, for 5 to 10 minutes before serving.

12. To serve, remove the corn husks from the tamales. Top with shredded lettuce and ladle about ⅓ cup of the warmed tomato sauce or salsa over each tamale. Enjoy!

Make-ahead tip: Because making tamales can be time consuming, the best and easiest way is to prepare the filling 2 days in advance, and the masa 1 day in advance. Soak the corn husks in the morning on the day you want to serve the tamales, and then all you'll have to do is assemble them.

Cochinita Pibil

PIBIL-STYLE PORK

PREP TIME: 10 minutes ✴ MANUAL: 30 minutes on high pressure ✴ RELEASE: Natural

TOTAL TIME: 50 minutes ✴ SERVES: 6 to 8 servings

It's so hard to choose just one favorite Mexican pork dish, especially with traditional dishes like *Cochinita Pibil*. This delicacy fit for the gods, which consists of roast pork wrapped in banana leaves, originated in the Yucatán Peninsula. This flavorful pork roast gets its delicious, tangy flavor from an achiote paste (or ground achiote) marinade made with vinegar and citrus juices. Enjoy *Cochinita Pibil* as a filling for tacos, quesadillas, and/or *tortas* (sandwiches).

2 ounces ground achiote

1¼ cups freshly squeezed
orange juice

½ cup freshly squeezed
lime juice

3 tablespoons white vinegar

3 garlic cloves, minced

2¼ pounds pork loin, cut into
2-inch pieces

1 teaspoon coarse salt

1 teaspoon ground cumin

½ teaspoon freshly ground
black pepper

½ teaspoon ground
cinnamon

½ teaspoon dried oregano

1 medium onion, thinly sliced

1 banana leaf

Warm corn tortillas, for
serving (optional)

Pickled Red Onions
(page 139), for garnish

1. In a medium glass bowl, mix together the ground achiote, orange juice, lime juice, vinegar, and garlic. Stir in the pork, mixing until completely coated with the marinade. Season with the salt, cumin, pepper, cinnamon, and oregano. Add the onion.

2. Transfer the pork mixture to the Instant Pot®.

3. On a comal or griddle, warm the banana leaf over medium-high heat for 2 to 3 minutes, turning occasionally, until soft and pliable; remove from the heat. Arrange the banana leaf on top of the pork mixture.

4. Lock the lid into place and set the steam release valve to sealed. Select Manual and set the timer for 30 minutes on high.

5. When cooking is complete, allow the pressure to release naturally. Unlock and remove the lid.

6. Carefully remove the banana leaf. Using two forks, shred the pork meat. Serve atop warm corn tortillas (if desired). Garnish with pickled red onions.

Substitution tip: This recipe can be made with chicken or jackfruit instead of pork. Reduce the cooking time to 15 minutes on high for chicken and 10 minutes on high for jackfruit.

Carne de Puerco con Chile

PORK IN CHILE SAUCE

PREP TIME: 10 minutes ✳ MANUAL: 30 minutes on high pressure ✳ RELEASE: Natural

TOTAL TIME: 1 hour 5 minutes ✳ SERVES: 6 to 8

This is a traditional dish popular in Los Altos de Jalisco (the highlands of Jalisco)—the place I called home for 18 years. It is made with juicy pieces of pork loin in a vibrant tomato, tomatillo, and árbol chile sauce. *Carne de Puerco* con Chile was one of my *suegra*'s signature dishes, and it became one of my all-time favorites to make when the whole family would get together. This recipe, which I've adapted for the Instant Pot®, calls for 1½ cups of the tomatillo and árbol chile salsa, but to turn the heat down, feel free to reduce the amount to 1 cup and increase the *Caldillo de Jitomate* to 3 cups.

2 tablespoons *manteca* (pork lard) or vegetable oil

2¼ pounds pork loin, cut into 2-inch pieces

1½ teaspoons coarse salt

½ teaspoon freshly ground black pepper

½ medium white onion

4 garlic cloves, minced

6 cilantro sprigs

2 cups *Caldillo de Jitomate* (page 16) or tomato sauce

1½ cups Classic Tomatillo and Árbol Chile Salsa (page 18)

Frijoles Meneados (page 33), for serving (optional)

Ensalada de Nopales (Cactus Paddle Salad), for serving (see Option tip; optional)

Warm corn tortillas, for serving (optional)

1. Set the Instant Pot® to Sauté and adjust to More for high. Heat the *manteca* in the pot until completely melted. Add the pork loin and sauté, stirring occasionally, for 6 to 8 minutes, or until light golden brown. Season with the salt and pepper.

2. Add the onion, garlic, and cilantro. Stir in the tomato sauce, salsa, and 2 cups water.

3. Lock the lid into place and set the steam release valve to sealed. Select Manual and set the timer for 30 minutes on high.

4. When cooking is complete, allow the pressure to release naturally. Unlock and remove the lid.

5. Stir gently to combine. Serve with beans, salad, and warm corn tortillas (if desired).

Option tip: To make *Ensalada de Nopales*, mix together 1 pound of cooked, cooled, and chopped nopales with ½ cup chopped white onion, 1 cup diced tomatoes, 1 finely chopped serrano chile, and ¼ cup finely chopped fresh cilantro. Season with salt to taste.

Birria de Res

BEEF BIRRIA

PREP TIME: 10 minutes ✳ MANUAL: 45 minutes on high pressure ✳ RELEASE: Natural
TOTAL TIME: 1 hour 15 minutes ✳ SERVES: 6 to 8

Birria is a slow-roasted delicacy traditionally made with lamb or goat meat, but shredded beef is also an acceptable substitute. I like to prepare and serve mine the way it is made in Yahualica. The meat is simply roasted with onion, garlic, cilantro, salt, and pepper to enhance the flavor of the beef and the broth, which is then topped with Caldillo de Jitomate (page 16), chopped onion, and fresh serrano chiles for added heat. Oh, and don't forget the corn tortillas!

2½ to 3 pounds beef chuck roast or shanks

1½ teaspoons coarse salt

½ teaspoon freshly ground black pepper

½ teaspoon crushed dried Mexican oregano

1 medium onion, quartered

3 garlic cloves, thinly sliced

6 cilantro sprigs

2 dried bay leaves

3 to 4 cups Caldillo de Jitomate (page 16) or tomato sauce

Chopped white onion, for garnish

6 to 8 fresh serrano chiles, for garnish

Warm corn tortillas, for serving (optional)

1. If using beef chuck roast, cut into 2-inch slices and place inside the Instant Pot®. Season with salt, pepper, and oregano. Add the onion, garlic, cilantro, and bay leaves. Pour in 3 cups water.

2. Lock the lid into place and set the steam release valve to sealed. Select Manual and set the timer for 45 minutes on high.

3. When cooking is complete, allow the pressure to release naturally. Unlock and remove the lid. Remove and discard the bay leaves.

4. In a small saucepan, heat the tomato sauce over medium heat until simmering. Remove from the heat.

5. Discard the cilantro sprigs. Using two forks, shred the beef. To serve, spoon the desired amount of shredded beef into bowls. Ladle at least ⅓ cup each of the cooking broth and tomato sauce into each bowl. Garnish with chopped white onion. Serve with a fresh serrano chile on the side and plenty of warm corn tortillas (if desired).

Substitution tip: For authentic lamb birria, substitute 2½ to 3 pounds lamb shoulder roast for the beef chuck roast. Increase the cooking time to 60 minutes on high.

Tacos de Lengua

BEEF TONGUE TACOS

PREP TIME: 5 minutes ✳ MANUAL: 1 hour 10 minutes on high pressure

RELEASE: Natural ✳ TOTAL TIME: 1 hour 30 minutes ✳ SERVES: 10 to 12

I know what you're thinking . . . "Ew! Beef tongue tacos! I can't!" I get it. I used to be the same way. *Lengua* (tongue) is not the prettiest cut of meat at the butcher shop, and depending on how it's sliced, it can have an iffy texture. But when cooked just right, *lengua* is melt-in-your-mouth juicy and tender perfection. It's one of my favorite cuts of meat when I just want simple shredded (or roughly chopped) beef tacos. Tongue is my second favorite thing to cook in my Instant Pot®, because it comes out perfect every single time and you also get a rich, flavorful consommé (broth) to enjoy as well. One of my favorite taquerias used to serve up Styrofoam cups filled with consommé garnished with chopped onion and cilantro, along with a squeeze of fresh lime juice.

1 (3½- to 4-pound) beef tongue

6 cilantro sprigs

½ medium white onion, quartered

4 whole garlic cloves, peeled

2 serrano chiles, thinly sliced

1½ teaspoons coarse salt

1 teaspoon crushed dried Mexican oregano

½ teaspoon freshly ground black pepper

Corn tortillas, for serving

Chopped white onion, for garnish

Chopped fresh cilantro, for garnish

Lime wedges, for serving

Salsa, for serving

1. In the Instant Pot®, arrange the beef tongue and add 3 cups water. Add the cilantro, onion, garlic, and chiles. Season with the salt, oregano, and pepper.

2. Lock the lid into place and set the steam release valve to sealed. Select Manual and set the timer for 1 hour, 10 minutes on high.

3. When cooking is complete, allow the pressure to release naturally. Unlock and remove the lid.

4. Using a slotted spoon, transfer the cooked beef tongue to a cutting board. Discard the outer layer of skin. Roughly chop the tongue into bite-size pieces.

> CONTINUED

Tacos de Lengua

> CONTINUED

5. Heat the corn tortillas on a comal or griddle over medium heat until soft and pliable. Stack two corn tortillas per taco. Spoon 2 to 3 heaping tablespoons of chopped beef tongue down the center of each tortilla stack. Garnish with chopped onion and cilantro. Serve with lime wedges and your favorite salsa.

Option tip: Don't let the cooking broth from the *lengua* go to waste! Strain and ladle it into bowls or coffee mugs. Garnish with chopped onion and cilantro. Top with a squeeze of fresh lime juice. Enjoy!

Mole Pulled Pork Sliders

PREP TIME: 10 minutes ✳ **SAUTÉ:** 5 minutes ✳ **MANUAL:** 30 minutes on high pressure
RELEASE: Natural ✳ **TOTAL TIME:** 1 hour 10 minutes ✳ **SERVES:** 6 to 8

Store-bought mole paste is a must in my Mexican pantry. I use it as a rich and delicious sauce for everything from pizzas to empanadas to these delectable sliders. These are the perfect finger food to serve at your next sporting event or family get-together. Served on toasted Hawaiian rolls and garnished with pickled red onions, these sliders are a fun twist on classic *tacos de mole*.

2 tablespoons vegetable oil

1 (8.25-ounce) jar mole paste
(I use Doña María brand)

2 cups chicken broth

6 tablespoons sugar

1 teaspoon coarse salt

½ teaspoon freshly ground
black pepper

¼ teaspoon ground cloves

¼ teaspoon ground
cinnamon

2¼ pounds pork loin, cut into
3- to 4-inch pieces

Hawaiian rolls, for serving

Pickled Red Onions
(page 139), for garnish

1. Set the Instant Pot® to Sauté and adjust to More for high. Heat the vegetable oil in the pot. Stir in the mole paste, stirring constantly for 3 to 5 minutes, or until completely melted into the oil. Whisk in the chicken broth and 2 cups water until completely combined into a velvety sauce. Season with the sugar, salt, pepper, cloves, and cinnamon. Add the pork loin, making sure each piece is coated with the mole sauce.

2. Lock the lid into place and set the steam release valve to sealed. Select Manual and set the timer for 30 minutes on high.

3. When cooking is complete, allow the pressure to release naturally. Unlock and remove the lid.

4. Using two forks, shred the pork loin. Split the Hawaiian rolls in half crosswise. On a comal or griddle, toast the rolls over medium heat for 2 to 3 minutes, or until light golden brown. Spoon 2 or 3 heaping tablespoons of the mole pulled pork onto the bottom half of each roll. Garnish with pickled onions. Set the top half of the rolls in place and serve.

Option tip: Round out your menu with a basketful of tortilla chips and Queso Blanco Dip (page 17)!

ARROZ CON TRES LECHES, PAGE 122

CHAPTER 8

Sweets & Desserts

Arroz con Tres Leches

MEXICAN THREE-MILK RICE PUDDING

PREP TIME: 5 minutes ✳ **MANUAL:** 20 minutes on high pressure ✳ **RELEASE:** Natural
TOTAL TIME: 50 minutes ✳ **SERVES:** 6

Arroz con leche is a sweet and creamy Mexican rice pudding lightly infused with cinnamon that both kids and grown-ups love. This version is extra creamy because it is made *tres leches*–style, with three types of milk: whole, evaporated, and sweetened condensed. Using the Instant Pot® for this classic Mexican dessert makes it even easier to enjoy with no hassle at all. Just mix in the ingredients, cover the pot, press start, and forget about it.

3 cups whole milk

1 (14-ounce) can sweetened condensed milk

1 (10-ounce) can evaporated milk

⅛ teaspoon coarse salt

1 cup long-grain rice

2 (3-inch) cinnamon sticks

Ground cinnamon, for serving

1. In the Instant Pot®, combine the whole milk, condensed milk, evaporated milk, and 2 cups water, whisking until combined. Season with the salt.

2. Add the rice and cinnamon sticks.

3. Lock the lid into place and set the steam release valve to sealed. Select Manual and set the timer for 20 minutes on high.

4. When cooking is complete, allow the pressure to release naturally. Unlock and remove the lid.

5. Discard the cinnamon sticks. Gently stir the rice to combine. Serve warm; sprinkle with ground cinnamon just before serving.

Option tip: Rice pudding can also be enjoyed cold. Simply allow *arroz con leche* to cool completely, then transfer to an airtight container, cover, and refrigerate for at least two hours before serving. Top with a dollop of whipped cream and sprinkle with ground cinnamon.

Atole de Avena

MEXICAN OATMEAL

PREP TIME: 5 minutes ✳ MANUAL: 20 minutes on high pressure ✳ RELEASE: Natural
TOTAL TIME: 50 minutes ✳ SERVES: 6 to 8

Atole is a deliciously sweet Mexican porridge that can be thickened with cornstarch, masa harina, or, in the case of Atole de Avena, oats. This creamy Mexican oatmeal, simmered in milk with cinnamon, is traditionally served in mugs to sip slowly to keep you warm on a cold winter's day. In Mexico it is common to enjoy Atole de Avena for breakfast or a late-night snack with a piece of *pan dulce* (Mexican pastry).

4 cups whole milk
⅛ teaspoon coarse salt
½ to ¾ cup sugar
1 cup old-fashioned oats
2 (3-inch) cinnamon sticks, plus more for garnish

1. In the Instant Pot®, whisk together 3 cups water, the milk, salt, and sugar until the sugar has completely dissolved. Stir in the oats and cinnamon sticks.

2. Lock the lid into place and set the steam release valve to sealed. Select Manual and set the timer for 20 minutes on high.

3. When cooking is complete, allow the pressure to release naturally. Unlock and remove the lid.

4. Discard the cinnamon sticks. Stir the oatmeal gently to combine. Ladle into mugs. Garnish with more cinnamon sticks.

Option tip: Transform this oatmeal into a chocolaty treat by stirring in 1 (3-ounce) tablet of Mexican chocolate with the ingredients in step 1. The chocolate will melt as the oatmeal cooks.

Café de Olla

MEXICAN COFFEE

PREP TIME: 5 minutes ✳ MANUAL: 15 minutes on high pressure ✳ RELEASE: Natural
TOTAL TIME: 40 minutes ✳ SERVES: 8

Wake up your taste buds with this fragrant Mexican coffee known as Café de Olla (coffee from a pot). My grandparents made it often, and their recipe simply included coffee, cinnamon, and piloncillo (unrefined cane sugar). Over the years, I've added a few spices like star anise and cloves to intensify the flavors of the coffee and cinnamon. Sometimes I like to add a little orange zest to the mix for a lingering citrus undertone.

¼ cup ground Mexican coffee (I use Café Legal brand)

2 (3-inch) cinnamon sticks, plus more for garnish

2 whole star anise

8 whole cloves

1 piloncillo cone (see Ingredient tip, page 126)

1 tablespoon finely grated orange zest (optional)

¼ to ½ cup granulated sugar (optional)

1. In the Instant Pot®, combine 8 cups water, the coffee, and 2 cinnamon sticks.

2. Stir in the star anise, cloves, piloncillo cone, and orange zest (if using).

3. Lock the lid into place and set the steam release valve to sealed. Select Manual and set the timer for 15 minutes on high.

4. When cooking is complete, allow the pressure to release naturally. Unlock and remove the lid.

5. Discard the cinnamon sticks; stir the coffee gently to combine. Sweeten with the granulated sugar (if using). Strain the coffee into mugs. Garnish with cinnamon sticks.

Option: Café de olla is traditionally served black, but you can add a splash of milk, coffee creamer, coffee liqueur, or even Bailey's Irish Cream, if desired.

Champurrado

MEXICAN HOT CHOCOLATE PORRIDGE

PREP TIME: 5 minutes * **MANUAL:** 8 minutes on high pressure * **RELEASE:** Natural
TOTAL TIME: 35 minutes * **SERVES:** 6

Champurrado is another popular Mexican *atole* (porridge), made with Mexican chocolate and thickened with masa harina, which gives it a grainy texture. Champurrado is a thicker version of Mexican chocolate. It's warm, comforting, and always reminds me of my childhood. It is delicious served with a piece of your favorite Mexican *pan dulce* or with tamales for a complete breakfast.

3 cups whole milk

½ cup masa harina

1 (3 ounce) tablet Mexican chocolate, cut into eighths

1 (3-inch) cinnamon stick, plus more for garnish

½ cup sugar, divided

1. In a blender, purée the milk, masa harina, and 3 cups water until smooth. Pour into the Instant Pot®.

2. Add the Mexican chocolate, cinnamon stick, and ¼ cup of sugar, stirring until the sugar is completely dissolved.

3. Lock the lid into place and set the steam release valve to sealed. Select Manual and set the timer for 8 minutes on high.

4. When cooking is complete, allow the pressure to release naturally. Unlock and remove the lid.

5. Discard the cinnamon stick. Stir the *champurrado* gently to combine. Sweeten with the remaining ¼ cup sugar, if desired. Ladle into mugs. Garnish with cinnamon sticks.

Ingredient tip: Masa harina, the ground corn flour used to thicken Champurrado, is used to make corn tortillas and *masa* (dough) for tamales, and can also be used to thicken soups, stews, and chilies.

Camotes Enmielados

CANDIED YAMS

PREP TIME: 5 minutes ✳ MANUAL: 25 minutes on high pressure ✳ RELEASE: Natural
TOTAL TIME: 55 minutes ✳ SERVES: 6 to 8

This is a Mexican delicacy similar to candied yams. The *camotes* (sweet potatoes) simmer in water topped with cinnamon sticks, while the piloncillo cones melt atop them into a rich, thick cinnamon-infused syrup. Unlike candied yams, Camotes Enmielados aren't just for the holidays. They can be enjoyed year-round, eaten for breakfast with a tall glass of milk or as an after-dinner dessert. My favorite way to enjoy Camotes Enmielados is in a bowl with lots of the sticky-sweet syrup and a splash (or two) of ice-cold milk poured right on top.

2¼ pounds sweet potatoes, cut into 2-inch slices
2 (3-inch) cinnamon sticks
2 piloncillo cones (see Ingredient tip)

1. In the Instant Pot®, combine the sweet potatoes and 2 cups water. Top with the cinnamon sticks and piloncillo cones.

2. Lock the lid into place and set the steam release valve to sealed. Select Manual and set the timer for 25 minutes on high.

3. When cooking is complete, allow the pressure to release naturally. Unlock and remove the lid. Serve immediately.

Ingredient tip: Piloncillo is unrefined cane sugar that is shaped into cones. You can find it in the produce section of your local Hispanic supermarket.

Capirotada

MEXICAN BREAD PUDDING

PREP TIME: 10 minutes ✳ SAUTÉ: 8 minutes ✳ MANUAL: 10 minutes on high pressure
RELEASE: Quick ✳ TOTAL TIME: 30 minutes ✳ SERVES: 6 to 8

Another memorable sweet treat from my childhood is Capirotada, a sweet and simple Mexican bread pudding made with layers of golden-fried bolillo roll slices, raisins, and queso fresco in a piloncillo-and-cinnamon–infused syrup. Traditionally, Capirotada is served during the Catholic celebration of Cuaresma (Lent), as all of the ingredients are representative of the crucifixion. The bread symbolizes the body of Christ, the syrup His blood, the cloves are the nails of the cross, and the cheese is the shroud that covered Christ's body. Capirotada is also popular during the holiday season, although I could eat this scrumptious dessert all year long.

2 piloncillo cones (see Ingredient tip, page 126)

2 (3-inch) cinnamon sticks

4 whole cloves

4 tablespoons vegetable oil, divided

4 day-old bolillo rolls, cut into 1-inch slices

1 cup peanuts, divided

½ cup raisins, divided

1½ cups crumbled queso fresco, divided

1. In a medium saucepan, combine the piloncillo cones, cinnamon sticks, cloves, and 2 cups of water. Bring to a boil over high heat; cover and reduce the heat to low. Simmer, stirring occasionally, until the piloncillo cones dissolve completely. Remove from the heat.

2. Set the Instant Pot® to Sauté and adjust to More for high. Heat 2 tablespoons of vegetable oil in the pot. Working in two or three batches, fry the bolillo roll slices for 2 to 3 minutes, flipping once, until light golden brown on both sides. Repeat until all the bread slices are evenly golden, adding the remaining 2 tablespoons of vegetable oil as needed.

> CONTINUED

Capirotada

> CONTINUED

3. In the Instant Pot®, layer half of the toasted bolillo slices. Top with half each of the piloncillo syrup, peanuts, raisins, and queso fresco. Repeat the layering one more time.

4. Lock the lid into place and set the steam release valve to sealed. Select Manual and set the timer for 10 minutes on high.

5. When cooking is complete, quick release the pressure. Unlock and remove the lid. Serve immediately.

Option tip: With just a few additions to the layers of bolillo slices and raisins, you can create fun and tasty versions of Capirotada. For a banana-nut Capirotada, add 3 sliced bananas and 1 cup pecan halves; drizzle with Mexican cajeta (caramel sauce) before serving. Or, for an apple pie Capirotada, add in 3 thinly sliced Granny Smith apples and substitute Cheddar cheese for the queso fresco; drizzle with maple syrup before serving.

Capirotada de Leche

MEXICAN BREAD PUDDING WITH MILK

KID-FRIENDLY

VEGETARIAN

PREP TIME: 10 minutes ✳ **MANUAL:** 15 minutes on high pressure ✳ **RELEASE:** Natural
TOTAL TIME: 45 minutes ✳ **SERVES:** 4 to 6

Another popular bread pudding in Mexico is Capirotada de Leche. This is a milk-based bread pudding made with Mexican pan dulce in a simple custard. Kids love it because it's made with *conchas*—soft, billowy Mexican pastries with a colorful sugar topping—then topped with brightly colored sprinkles and a drizzle of sweetened condensed milk for added sweetness. You'll love how quickly and easily this dessert comes together.

4 large eggs
3 cups whole milk
½ cup sugar
1 teaspoon vanilla extract
Nonstick cooking spray
4 Mexican *conchas* (1 pink,
   1 yellow, 1 white, and
   1 chocolate)
4 tablespoons colored
   sprinkles
Sweetened condensed milk,
   for serving (optional)

1. In a blender, purée the eggs, milk, sugar, and vanilla until smooth.

2. Spray the inside of the Instant Pot® with cooking spray. Layer in half each of the *conchas*, custard purée, and sprinkles. Repeat the layers one more time.

3. Lock the lid into place and set the steam release valve to sealed. Select Manual and set the timer for 15 minutes on high.

4. When cooking is complete, allow the pressure to release naturally. Unlock and remove the lid.

5. Serve immediately, drizzled with sweetened condensed milk (if desired).

Option tip: Transform this dessert into a rich, buttery, chocolaty dream by substituting croissants for the *conchas*, omitting the colored sprinkles, and adding 1½ cups of dark chocolate chips to the layers.

SWEETS & DESSERTS   129

GUACAMOLE, PAGE 137

CHAPTER 9

Sides & Staples

Tortillas de Maíz

CORN TORTILLAS

PREP TIME: 5 minutes   ✳   COOK TIME: 25 minutes   ✳   TOTAL TIME: 30 minutes

MAKES: 12 tortillas

Like in my previous cookbook, many of the recipes included throughout this book can be served as fillings for tacos. But to make tacos, tortillas are a must. And what better way to host an authentic Mexican feast than with homemade corn tortillas? All you need is a little masa harina! Masa harina is a finely ground corn flour made from nixtamalized corn, and it's used to make dough for tortillas, tamales, *sopes*, and *gorditas*. Depending on how many tortillas you need, this recipe can be easily doubled or tripled.

2 cups masa harina (I use Maseca brand)

¼ teaspoon coarse salt

1¼ cups plus 2 tablespoons warm water or chicken broth

1. Heat a comal or griddle over medium heat. In a medium bowl, mix together the masa harina, salt, and 1¼ cups of warm water until the dough comes together and is smooth. If the dough is too dry or crumbly, stir in more water, 1 tablespoon at a time, until it is the desired consistency.

2. Divide the dough into 12 (1½-inch) balls. Using a tortilla press lined with plastic wrap or parchment paper, flatten each ball of dough into a 6-inch circle. If you do not own a tortilla press, place a ball of masa between two pieces of plastic wrap or parchment paper, then flatten with a large, heavy plate.

3. Cook each tortilla on the comal or griddle for 45 to 60 seconds per side, or until cooked through and starting to fill with air. As each tortilla finishes cooking, remove from the heat, transfer to a plate, and keep warm by covering with a clean kitchen towel. Repeat with the remaining masa to make a total of 12 tortillas.

Option tip: Save a few minutes in the kitchen by using a 1-pound bag of ready-made tortilla masa from your local Hispanic supermarket. Store in a plastic zip-top bag, keep refrigerated, and use as needed.

Masa Harina Cornbread

PREP TIME: 5 minutes ✳ COOK TIME: 25 minutes ✳ TOTAL TIME: 30 minutes

SERVES: 8

I don't know about you, but whenever I think about the chili recipes in this cookbook, I get a craving for homemade cornbread. While living in Mexico, I did not have access to cornmeal, but sometimes I still craved the buttery goodness of cornbread, so I found a way to recreate a childhood favorite using ingredients I had in my pantry. And that is how this masa harina cornbread was born.

1 cup masa harina (I use Maseca brand)
1 cup all-purpose flour
2 tablespoons sugar
1 teaspoon coarse salt
1 teaspoon baking powder
½ teaspoon baking soda
1 cup buttermilk
2 large eggs
2 tablespoons vegetable oil
4 tablespoons (1 stick) butter, divided

1. Preheat the oven to 350° F.

2. In a mixing bowl, combine the masa harina, flour, sugar, salt, baking powder, and baking soda. Stir in the buttermilk, eggs, and vegetable oil until well combined; set aside.

3. Melt 3 tablespoons of butter in an 8-inch ovenproof or cast iron skillet over low heat. Remove from the heat and pour in the batter. (Do not stir!)

4. Bake the cornbread at 350°F for 20 to 25 minutes, or until light golden brown and a toothpick inserted in the center comes out clean. Remove from the oven and spread the remaining 1 tablespoon of butter on top of the cornbread. Enjoy!

Option tip: Add more flavor to your cornbread by stirring in any (or all) of the following ingredients: a small can of roasted green chiles; a small can of drained golden corn kernels; 1 cup finely chopped deli ham; and/or 1½ cups shredded Cheddar or Colby Jack cheese.

Roasted Poblano Peppers

PREP TIME: 5 minutes ✳ COOK TIME: 15 minutes ✳ TOTAL TIME: 20 minutes

SERVES: 6 to 8

These roasted peppers are the base of dishes like Tacos Rajas con Crema (page 64), but they can also be stirred into various soups and stews for added flavor. Poblano peppers are large dark-green chiles not really known for packing a lot of heat, but sometimes you might encounter a spicy one. The easiest way to roast poblano peppers is over an open flame on the stove top, but if you have an electric stove, you can roast them on a comal or nonstick skillet.

8 poblano peppers

1. Roast the peppers, two at a time, over an open flame on high heat, turning occasionally, until completely charred all over.

2. Place the roasted peppers in a plastic bag and wrap tightly. Let sit for about 10 minutes. (This allows the chiles to sweat, making it much easier to remove the charred skin.)

3. Using a butter knife, scrape off and discard the charred skin. Remove the stems and seeds from the chiles. Cut the chiles into thin slices. Refrigerate in an airtight container until ready to use.

Technique tip: It's important to remember to wear plastic or latex gloves when working with raw chiles to prevent a burning sensation on your hands. Should your skin come in direct contact with the roasted chiles or seeds, simply wash your hands with a little dish soap and baking soda to form a paste. Let the paste dry for one minute before rinsing off.

Pico de Gallo Verde

PREP TIME: 15 minutes, plus 1 hour to chill ✷ MAKES: 1½ cups

Everyone knows and loves pico de gallo, that delicious Mexican salsa made with fresh ingredients in the colors of the Mexican flag. But did you know that there is more than one way to enjoy it? One of my favorite versions of this Mexican classic is Pico de Gallo Verde, made with tomatillos, serrano chiles, red onion, cilantro, and lime juice. Serve this salsa with grilled meats, over nachos, or with a never-ending basket of tortilla chips for dipping.

1 pound tomatillos, husks removed, finely chopped

½ medium red onion, finely chopped

3 serrano chiles, finely chopped

¼ cup finely chopped fresh cilantro

Juice of 2 limes

Coarse salt

1. In a medium bowl, mix together the tomatillos, onion, chiles, and cilantro. Add the lime juice. Season with salt.

2. Cover with plastic wrap and refrigerate for at least 1 hour before serving.

Substitution tip: If spicy foods are not your friend, substitute 1 seeded Anaheim chile for the serrano chiles. You'll get the all the flavor of a green chile without the heat.

Nopales

PREP TIME: 5 minutes ✳ COOK TIME: 15 minutes ✳ TOTAL TIME: 20 minutes

SERVES: 4 to 6

Nopales, which are the leaves (a.k.a. cactus paddles) of the prickly pear cactus, are a staple ingredient in Mexican cuisine. Loaded with vitamins and minerals, nopales can be boiled, grilled, or even sautéed, which is my preferred method, as it eliminates the viscous liquid known in Spanish as *babas* (slime). Nopales can be enjoyed on their own, as part of a refreshing salad, or stirred into your favorite soups and stews.

1 pound nopales, thorns removed and thinly sliced

¼ medium white onion, thinly sliced

2 or 3 cilantro sprigs

Coarse salt

1. In a medium nonstick skillet, combine the nopales, onion, and cilantro. Season lightly with coarse salt. (Do not add water or oil.)

2. Sauté over medium heat until the nopales start to release their natural liquid.

3. Cover the skillet and reduce the heat to low. Let the nopales simmer, stirring occasionally, for 10 to 12 minutes, or until completely cooked through and all the liquid has evaporated.

4. Serve the nopales immediately or let cool slightly.

Ingredient tip: Fresh cactus paddles are easy to find at your local Hispanic supermarket and can be bought already cleaned (thorns removed), as well as sliced or chopped. When buying whole cactus paddles, search for small to medium-size nopales, as the larger ones can be tougher and take longer to cook.

Guacamole

MAKES: 2 cups ✳ PREP TIME: 15 minutes

Nobody can resist a bowlful of guacamole, especially if there are tortilla chips nearby for dipping! Sure, you can buy the store-bought stuff, but nothing else really compares to the flavor of homemade guacamole. And your friends or guests will be super impressed with your knowledge of Mexican cuisine when they see you making guacamole from scratch.

3 ripe avocados, halved
   and pitted
2 Roma tomatoes, seeded
   and finely chopped
¼ medium red onion,
   finely chopped
1 to 2 serrano chiles,
   finely chopped
¼ cup finely chopped
   fresh cilantro
¼ cup Mexican crema or
   sour cream (optional)
Coarse salt

1. Scoop out the flesh of the avocados into a medium bowl. Lightly mash with a potato masher or fork.

2. Stir in the tomatoes, onion, chiles, cilantro, and Mexican crema (if using). Season with salt.

3. Cover the guacamole tightly with plastic wrap. Refrigerate until ready to serve.

Ingredient tip: Exposure to air (oxygen) is what causes guacamole to brown. To prevent this from happening, always keep guacamole wrapped tightly with plastic. If the guacamole starts to brown, just scrape off the darkened part with a spoon.

Salsa de Pepino

CUCUMBER SALSA

PREP TIME: 10 minutes ✳ MAKES: 2½ to 3 cups

This refreshing cucumber salsa was a new discovery for me upon moving to Mexico. It is often served as a garnish for traditional pork pozole. Made with finely chopped fresh cucumber, red onion, cilantro, and lime juice, the base of this recipe is made with my favorite Classic Tomatillo and Árbol Chile Salsa (page 18). This salsa is good for more than just stirring into pozole. It's delicious served atop ceviche tostadas or grilled meats, or with tortillas chips.

1 medium cucumber, peeled, seeded, and finely chopped

½ medium red onion, finely chopped

¼ cup finely chopped fresh cilantro

Juice of 2 limes

Coarse salt

1½ cups Classic Tomatillo and Árbol Chile Salsa (page 18)

1. In a medium bowl, combine the cucumber, red onion, and cilantro. Add the lime juice. Season with salt.

2. Stir in the salsa and mix well. Cover and refrigerate until ready to serve.

Option tip: A fun way to turn this salsa into a spicy appetizer is to stir in 1 pound of cooked and cooled shrimp that has already been peeled and deveined. Spoon onto tostada shells and garnish with slices of avocado.

Pickled Red Onions

PREP TIME: 5 minutes, plus 2 hours to rest ✳ MAKES: 2 cups

At the risk of repeating recipes from my taco cookbook, one recipe worth also including in this book are these pickled red onions. They are the perfect garnish to so many recipes, including the Mole Pulled Pork Sliders (page 119). This recipe couldn't be easier, and I'm sure you'll agree that it really was worthy of being repeated.

2 medium red onions,
  thinly sliced
2 to 3 serrano chiles,
  finely chopped
Coarse salt
Juice of 6 limes

1. In a medium bowl, combine the red onions and serrano chiles. Season with salt.

2. Add the lime juice and mix well. Cover tightly and refrigerate for at least 2 hours before serving. The onions will turn a bright-pink color when pickled.

Substitution tip: Increase the heat by substituting habaneros for the serrano chiles.

Fruity Agua Fresca

PREP TIME: 10 minutes ✴ SERVES: 12 to 16

No Mexican-inspired feast would be complete without a few pitchers of ice-cold Fruity Agua Fresca. Made with fresh fruit, water, and sugar, you can enjoy a refreshing glass of Agua Fresca with whatever fruit is in season. Some of my favorite fruits to use are strawberries, pineapple, watermelon, cantaloupe, bananas, papaya, mangos, and guavas, just to name a few.

6 cups fresh fruit, peeled
  if necessary
¾ to 1 cup sugar

1. In a blender, purée the fruit with 6 cups of water until smooth, working in batches if necessary.

2. Strain the fruit purée into a 4-quart (1-gallon) pitcher. Sweeten with the sugar to taste. Pour in enough water to fill the pitcher. Chill in the refrigerator until ready to serve.

3. Serve over ice.

Option tip: Transform your Agua Fresca into a fruity colada by omitting the sugar and stirring in a 14-ounce can of sweetened condensed milk. Your fruity coladas can be made into a quick and easy grown-up cocktail by adding a shot of tequila, rum, or vodka to each glass before serving.

"No Mexican-inspired feast would be complete without a few pitchers of ice-cold Fruity Agua Fresca."

Grains

To prevent foaming, it's best to rinse these grains thoroughly before cooking, or include a small amount of butter or oil with the cooking liquid.

	Liquid per 1 Cup of Grains	Minutes under Pressure	Pressure	Release
Arborio (or other medium-grain) rice	1½ cups	6	High	Quick
Barley, pearled	2½ cups	10	High	Natural
Brown rice, medium-grain	1½ cups	6–8	High	Natural
Brown rice, long-grain	1½ cups	13	High	Natural for 10 minutes, then quick
Buckwheat	1¾ cups	2–4	High	Natural
Farro, pearled	2 cups	6–8	High	Natural
Farro, whole-grain	3 cups	22–24	High	Natural
Oats, rolled	3 cups	3–4	High	Quick
Oats, steel-cut	4 cups	12	High	Natural
Quinoa	2 cups	2	High	Quick
Wheat berries	2 cups	30	High	Natural for 10 minutes, then quick
White rice, long-grain	1½ cups	3	High	Quick
Wild rice	2½ cups	18–20	High	Natural

Beans and Legumes

When cooking beans, if you have a pound or more, it's best to use low pressure and increase the cooking time by a minute or two (with larger amounts, there's more chance for foaming at high pressure). If you have less than a pound, high pressure is fine. A little oil in the cooking liquid will reduce foaming.

Unless a shorter release time is indicated, let the pressure release naturally for at least 15 minutes, after which any remaining pressure can be quick-released.

	Minutes under Pressure (Unsoaked)	Minutes under Pressure (Soaked in salted water)	Pressure	Release
Black beans	22	10	High	Natural
	25	12	Low	
Black-eyed peas	12	5	High	Natural for 8 minutes, then quick
	15	7	Low	
Cannellini beans	25	8	High	Natural
	28	10	Low	
Chickpeas (garbanzo beans)	18	3	High	Natural for 3 minutes, then quick
	20	4	Low	
Kidney beans	25	8	High	Natural
	28	10	Low	
Lentils	10	not recommended	High	Quick
Lima beans	15	4	High	Natural for 5 minutes, then quick
	18	5	Low	
Navy beans	18	8	High	Natural
	20	10	Low	
Pinto beans	25	10	High	Natural
	28	12	Low	
Split peas (unsoaked)	5 (firm peas) to 8 (soft peas)	not recommended	High	Natural
Soy beans, fresh (edamame)	1	not recommended	High	Quick
Soybeans, dried	25	12	High	Natural
	28	14	Low	

Meat

Except when noted, these times are for braised meats—that is, meats that are seared before pressure cooking and partially submerged in liquid.

	Minutes under Pressure	Pressure	Release
Beef, bone-in short ribs	40	High	Natural
Beef, flat iron steak, cut into ½" strips	1	Low	Quick
Beef, sirloin steak, cut into ½" strips	1	Low	Quick
Beef, shoulder (chuck) roast (2 lb)	35	High	Natural
Beef, shoulder (chuck), 2" chunks	20	High	Natural for 10 minutes
Lamb, shanks	35–40	High	Natural
Lamb, shoulder, 2" chunks	15–20	High	Natural
Pork, shoulder roast (2 lb)	25	High	Natural
Pork, shoulder, 2" chunks	20	High	Natural
Pork, back ribs (steamed)	30	High	Quick
Pork, spare ribs (steamed)	20	High	Quick
Pork, smoked sausage, ½" slices	20	High	Quick
Pork, tenderloin	4	Low	Quick

Poultry

Except when noted, these times are for braised poultry—that is, partially submerged in liquid.

	Minutes under Pressure	Pressure	Release
Chicken breast, bone-in (steamed)	8	Low	Natural for 5 minutes
Chicken breast, boneless (steamed)	5	Low	Natural for 8 minutes
Chicken thigh, bone-in	15	High	Natural for 10 minutes
Chicken thigh, boneless	8	High	Natural for 10 minutes
Chicken thigh, boneless, 1"–2" pieces	5	High	Quick
Chicken, whole (seared on all sides)	12–14	Low	Natural for 8 minutes
Duck quarters, bone-in	35	High	Quick
Turkey breast, tenderloin (12 oz) (steamed)	5	Low	Natural for 8 minutes
Turkey thigh, bone-in	30	High	Natural

Vegetables

The cooking method for all the following vegetables is steaming; if the vegetables are cooked in liquid, the times may vary. Green vegetables will be tender-crisp; root vegetables will be soft.

	Prep	Minutes under Pressure	Pressure	Release
Acorn squash	Halved	9	High	Quick
Artichokes, large	Whole	15	High	Quick
Beets	Quartered if large; halved if small	9	High	Natural
Broccoli	Cut into florets	1	Low	Quick
Brussels sprouts	Halved	2	High	Quick
Butternut squash	Peeled, ½" chunks	8	High	Quick
Cabbage	Sliced	5	High	Quick
Carrots	½"–1" slices	2	High	Quick
Cauliflower	Cut into florets	1	Low	Quick
Cauliflower	Whole	6	High	Quick
Green beans	Cut in half or thirds	1	Low	Quick
Potatoes, large, russet (for mashing)	Quartered	8	High	Natural for 8 minutes, then quick
Potatoes, red	Whole if less than 1½" across, halved if larger	4	High	Quick
Spaghetti squash	Halved lengthwise	7	High	Quick
Sweet potatoes	Halved lengthwise	8	High	Natural

MEASUREMENT CONVERSIONS

Volume Equivalents (Liquid)

Standard	US Standard (ounces)	Metric (approximate)
2 tablespoons	1 fl. oz.	30 mL
¼ cup	2 fl. oz.	60 mL
½ cup	4 fl. oz.	120 mL
1 cup	8 fl. oz.	240 mL
1½ cups	12 fl. oz.	355 mL
2 cups or 1 pint	16 fl. oz.	475 mL
4 cups or 1 quart	32 fl. oz.	1 L
1 gallon	128 fl. oz.	4 L

Oven Temperatures

Fahrenheit (F)	Celsius (C) (approximate)
250°F	120°C
300°F	150°C
325°F	165°C
350°F	180°C
375°F	190°C
400°F	200°C
425°F	220°C
450°F	230°C

Volume Equivalents (Dry)

Standard	Metric (approximate)
⅛ teaspoon	0.5 mL
¼ teaspoon	1 mL
½ teaspoon	2 mL
¾ teaspoon	4 mL
1 teaspoon	5 mL
1 tablespoon	15 mL
¼ cup	59 mL
⅓ cup	79 mL
½ cup	118 mL
⅔ cup	156 mL
¾ cup	177 mL
1 cup	235 mL
2 cups or 1 pint	475 mL
3 cups	700 mL
4 cups or 1 quart	1 L

Weight Equivalents

Standard	Metric (approximate)
½ ounce	15 g
1 ounce	30 g
2 ounces	60 g
4 ounces	115 g
8 ounces	225 g
12 ounces	340 g
16 ounces or 1 pound	455 g

THE DIRTY DOZEN AND THE CLEAN FIFTEEN™

A nonprofit environmental watchdog organization called Environmental Working Group (EWG) looks at data supplied by the U.S. Department of Agriculture (USDA) and the Food and Drug Administration (FDA) about pesticide residues. Each year it compiles a list of the best and worst pesticide loads found in commercial crops. You can use these lists to decide which fruits and vegetables to buy organic to minimize your exposure to pesticides and which produce is considered safe enough to buy conventionally. This does not mean they are pesticide-free, though, so wash these fruits and vegetables thoroughly.

Dirty Dozen	Clean Fifteen
apples	asparagus
celery	avocados
cherries	broccoli
grapes	cabbages
nectarines	cantaloupes
peaches	cauliflower
pears	eggplants
potatoes	honeydew melons
spinach	kiwis
strawberries	mangoes
sweet bell peppers	onions
tomatoes	papayas
	pineapples
	sweet corn
	sweet peas (frozen)

*Additionally, nearly three-quarters of hot pepper samples contained pesticide residues

RECIPE INDEX

INDEX

ABOUT THE AUTHOR

LESLIE HARRIS DE LIMÓN is the creator behind *La Cocina de Leslie* and author of *Taquería Tacos*. She was born and raised in Southern California, but lived in Mexico for 17 years. Surrounded by the foods her grandparents grew up eating in the Mexican states of Sonora and Chihuahua, she thought she knew just about everything there was to know about Mexican food. But it wasn't until she moved to Mexico that she learned that not all Mexican food is the same and that it varies from region to region. Her blog is more than just about Mexican food; it's a celebration of the rich culture and traditions of Mexico and her way of sharing memorable moments spent in *la cocina* with family and friends.

CPSIA information can be obtained
at www.ICGtesting.com
Printed in the USA
LVHW051711181118
597496LV00010B/12/P